Jesus
The Liberator of Desire

Jesus
the Liberator of Desire

SEBASTIAN MOORE

CROSSROAD · NEW YORK

1989

The Crossroad Publishing Company
370 Lexington Avenue, New York, N.Y. 10017

Copyright © 1989 by Sebastian Moore

Printed in the United States of America

Library of Congress Cataloging-in-Publication Data

Moore, Sebastian.
  Jesus the liberator of desire / Sebastian Moore.
    p.   cm.
  ISBN 0-8245-0939-0
  1. Jesus Christ—Person and offices. 2. Desire for God.
  3. Spiritual life—Catholic authors. I. Title.
  BT202.M565   1989
  248.4'82—dc19   89-485
                                                     CIP

For Chip Hughes
a true philosopher in this time

His beauty, ours entire,
Lifted them above sin,
Left them and lapped them in
Filling their hearts with fire.

Being all we may be
He took them beyond time,
Dropped them past power to climb,
Lifted them on his sea.

He is all beauty, whom
We see ourselves in now.
No doubt will he allow,
Left us an empty tomb.

Contents

Introduction

My aim in this book is to recover the image of the Crucified as meat and drink to the soul: Jesu joy of man's desiring. But what is desire? The clean opposite of the itch to which a debased Freudianism has reduced it, it is the allure of God. We are born into an overwhelming and unfathomable mystery that solicits us until we die. This solicitation is the primary meaning of desire. And when we try to understand this solicitation in the stages of our life, then the Freudian revolution sheds its reductionistic character and becomes a primary resource for this understanding; for it enables us to speak of the ego, formed out of the tension between oceanic oneness and the sense of being separate, and progressively re-formed as the sense of oneness and of individuality advance together toward the divine union.

It is in the interaction with Jesus, the man of oneness, that this liberation of desire into divine union takes place—normatively in the disciples of Jesus, of whose initial ecstasy, subsequent trauma, and coming thence into eternal life, the Christian Scriptures are the record. The search for an adequate account of the transformations of desire, that occupies the first chapters of this book, has for its aim an adequate account of *that* transformation of desire that took place in those whom Jesus pulled through a hideous experience. It seems to me, then, that the central question for an understanding of our salvation in Jesus Christ is: What is the death of ego

out of which we are brought into divine union? Such a
death of ego will, for the first time, relativize physical
death, dethrone it from its tragic reign. The answer to
the question is: that death of ego undergone by the
people Jesus had raised to the threshold of union by his
unique friendship, that death into which they were
thrown by his appalling end.

I have found this concentration on the followers of
Jesus illuminating of faith. It seems to me that a primary
theological need in our time is for the psychological to
mediate the transcendent. Until this comes about, the
psychological dimension remains subjective, the transcendent dimension extrinsic. The perennial vigor of
Christianity stems from a dangerous memory, of the
experience of a group of people being brought to a
crisis whose issue was such a freedom in face of our
mortality as can only come from the transcendent
ground of being. The psychological mediation of the
transcendent is *remembered*. Once this memory is recovered, the modern split between the Jesus of history
and the Christ of faith, which allows us to relegate
Christ as a symbol to the subjective sphere, vanishes. For
the dangerous memory is of the terrible moment out of
which the Jesus of history *became*, and for ever is, the
Christ of faith. To be awakened at this level is to have
one's answer to the common view that the Christian
myth has lost its power. The world to which the Christian story no longer speaks is a world in which individu-
alism has deadened the nerve of common hope that has
been unforgettably quickened, traumatized, and re-
enlivened with the joy of God.

Finally, I want to cheer up some of my fellow Catho-
lics, who are suffering a double oppression: of a worn-
out but still discouraging secularism, and of an ineptly
resumed ecclesiastical tyranny. Notwithstanding its en-

emies and its protectors, Catholic orthodoxy is a wildly beautiful thing. How could it not be, insisting as it does that God was crucified by our fear, to liberate our desire? The *London Tablet*'s editorial on *The Last Temptation of Christ* has it dead right when it says of theologians that their "task and duty is to show, to people today, that the most exciting thing, still, is Christian orthodoxy."

That is certainly what this book is trying to do.

PART ONE

Jesus as Liberator

1

Why Is There Why?

The question, Why is there anything? is a question about questioning. For it envisages all the questions that have ever been asked or that ever could be asked. It is the question, Why is there why? or, Why is there the why of things?

We have to ask this question, so it is a valid one. And to say that a question is valid is to say that it has an answer. But an answer to the question, Why is there the why of things? must be beyond our understanding. For it is the presupposed in all questions, the confidence in all questioning, that cannot be other than presupposed, that cannot be something we could discover, for all discoveries presuppose it. It insists on remaining in the background of our thinking. Bring it into the fore-ground, try to understand it, and it is no longer itself, for it belongs exclusively to the background, the presup-posed, the taken for granted.

This is the only access our mind has to the mystery we call God. And it is an immediate access that cannot be understood, that is, it cannot be the subject of an insight issuing in a verifiable hypothesis. Yet it is known in an intuitive wordless way, the way the background of our knowing is known.

3

Of this immediately known but not formulable answer to the question, Why is there the why of things? it
can and must be said that because of it all that is is. For it
is by definition the answer to the question, Why is there
anything at all?

Historically, as Eric Voegelin splendidly clarifies, the
first realization of the self as grounded in ultimate mystery took place in two ways, at the same time (about half
a millennium B.C.E.), in the two cultures respectively:
the Greek and the Hebrew. The Greek culture did it
"noetically," the Hebrew "pneumatically." The Greeks
did it by the kind of mental process I have just run
through. For the Hebrews it was more an experience of
the whole person, the spirit liberating humanity from its
enslavement to gods. In other words it was not just the
self as mind that emerged, but the self as free. But
generically, it is the same discovery, the same uncovering
of self. For as long as the gods are believed in, there are
whole areas of the world that we cannot hope to understand, areas subject to their caprice, so that asking questions about everything is held in check, with the further
consequence that the underlying question about all
questions cannot emerge. The Hebrews made this
breakthrough under the power of the spirit, manifest in
the great prophets of Israel.

Now because the experience of Israel was total, it
made a demand on the whole person to be faithful to
the transcendent reality, which in consequence took on a
strong personal character. "Thus says the Lord!" And
this brings us to our central problem: If the transcendent reality is personal, how can it still be the utterly
beyond-our-understanding, uncharacterizable reality
that it must be to be the answer to the question, Why is
there the why of things? I think everybody has this
problem, at different levels of articulation.

The Hebrew prophets were not unaware of this problem. The one thing they most deeply knew was that God could not be imagined. The only image of God is we ourselves, consciousness, the meaning of which is the infinite, the indefinable, the "background." This idea beautifully parallels the Greek "noetic" experience. Still, somehow the notion that God is an imaginable person is what came through the Hebraic account. "My ways are not your ways"—but they are "my" ways.

Wonderful things happened when the two streams came together in the Catholic Christian tradition. For then the "noetic" reminder that the answer is beyond our power to understand and name was able to question the enthusiastic statements of the "pneumatic" impulse that was only too ready to give it a personal name. The formulation of God as Trinity (the supreme achievement of this meeting of the Greek and Hebrew cultures) did mean that God was not *a* person, and suggested the beautiful idea of the transcendent as a mystery, an ineffable in-each-other-ness of "persons," into which we are drawn, rather than before which we are bowed down.

But still the job is not done—not nearly. Probably it is never done. Christianity today is bogged down in a failure to critique its utterances about the personal God in the light, equally divine, of the realization that the answer to Why *why?* must be beyond our comprehension. The Hebraic fervor urgently needs the Greek astringent, or we pull the divinity down to our level so that we cannot be pulled up to its level.

The overwhelming tendency is to say that in practice God is a person in a comprehensible sense, the Big Person who made the world, the Great Architect or Mathematician, and to provoke the atheistic philosopher to prove, quite correctly, that there can be no such person, since an expressed inexpressible, an effable ineffable, is a contradiction in terms. John Wisdom's parable of the Invisible Gardener who turns out on analysis to be nonexistent influenced generations of Oxford philosophers. Wisdom's god is a straw god. But I do not think intelligent people would have put such energy into his demolition if religious institutions were not putting a lot of energy into keeping him alive.

All this may sound very abstruse. But the effects of this treating the incomprehensible as though it were comprehensible, of talking about God as though God were somebody, are part of everybody's experience. Why does the word *God* somehow "not work"? Why do people's eyes glaze (piously) when they hear it? Because it is referring to that which is everything as though it were something. The word *God* has come to connote what I facetiously call the effable ineffable, the ultimate incomprehensible ground of all treated as comprehensible (and so becoming incomprehensible in a more colloquial sense), the self-contradictory description of the indescribable. The word *God* touches your and my intimate sense of ultimate mystery so that the mind begins to gestate, and then immediately aborts when it learns that we're supposed to know just what the word means.

This is a challenging and exciting situation. We are challenged to recover the excitement of our immediate awareness of the incomprehensible answer to Why is there why? And it is an immediate awareness—of the incomprehensible! That is not a contradiction. The thing we know with the greatest certainty is the mysteriousness of what underlies all our questioning. "If I could say what it is, it wouldn't be it," is an intuition, I think, that everyone has.

Einstein said a wonderfully provocative thing: "The most incomprehensible thing about the universe is that it is comprehensible." In other words, what blows the mind is that there is nothing that cannot be questioned in the hope of reaching an answer. The universality of why? provokes the deepest wonder, because it leads to the overwhelming question, Why is there why? to which the answer is an abyss of mystery with which we are strangely familiar.

Now the subject of this book is God as the liberation of desire. So we started by looking at desire and the abyss of Godhead in their essential relation. The desire for a full life stretches out to the infinite source of life in which we must become lost as, desiring to know life's meaning, we are lost in an answer that is mystery. This book is about this loss. It is about the lifelong process whereby our desire, at every crisis of growth, finds itself baffled by wanting something new that demands a change in ourselves, in who it is that wants. The meaning of this combination of new desire with breakdown in the desiring one is that surrender is the heart of our desirous relationship with the source of life—the surrender which we have already looked at in the clear mirror of the mind seeking to understand why anything is. The fulfillment, the full enactment of this combination of newly liberated desire with breakdown in the one who desires, is to be seen in the experience of the disciples of Jesus, men and women whom the God-in-man awoke to the full reach of desire, whom events brought to the final breakdown inherent in this dangerous growth, and proclaimed to an astonished world the birth of an age that will see no decline.

It may be useful, before we get going, to "fix" the intellectual version of the human story, so much easier to fix than the full existential reality, in some stanzas. We might preface these with a quote from Aquinas: "We do not know what Godhead is, we only know that it is, and that all that is depends on it."

I ask "Why is there anything?"
And know I have to ask,
And hence know that this questioning
Is an appropriate task.

Therefore there is an answer to
The question I have posed:
Then I reflect: My question too
Seeks to be diagnosed.

The questioning within the whole,
How can the answer be
Within the questioning's control?
Of this it must be free.

The question will direct my grasp
Toward the answer sought.
Asking of all, the sought will clasp
The questioner: I'm caught

In an abyss of mystery
Beyond all reckoning.
Nothing of it is known to me
Save "It grounds everything."

And all desire obeys this law,
Not just desire to know:
Desiring always to be more,
The more takes us in tow.

Why anything, O anything!
The question and the prayer
Alike throw us into the ring,
Its center everywhere.

2

The Theme

My theme is desire. To embark on this theme, I need an adequate account of self-awareness. Such an account will necessarily be corrective, and strongly so. For the culture that shapes our minds whether we will or no is systematically oblivious of what is at the heart of all self-awareness, namely the sense of being in a total reality, of "everything," of "the whole thing," of my life as adventure and event in a context that has no limits. Voegelin calls this dimension of consciousness "It-reality," the purpose of the term *It* being to conjure up the absolutely undifferentiated, that *in which* as opposed to that *which*. He contrasts this with "thing-reality." I must not labor the description. I must rather hope that you see, in your own experience, exactly what I am referring to.

To be self-aware *is* to be aware of myself *in* this total reality. Self-awareness cannot happen in isolation. I am aware of myself precisely *as* a relatedness. The notion of the self as an isolated monad is strictly meaningless, being deprived *ex professo* of what gives meaning, namely the whole mystery in which I am, in which, since the dawn of human time, I have dreamed up my myths. Our plight as a culture is desperate in that we think as though we were these unthinkable monads. When I love someone, monad A is sending a ping to monad B. It's

9

quite mad. Let us try to come out of the psychiatric ward of modernity into the clean air of what is.

This sense of being *in* the total mystery is necessarily a sense of *depending* on it. The very immediacy with which I feel myself, am "this sensible warm motion," accentuates the feeling of dependence. I often imagine myself about to do a parachute jump, as my turn in the lineup approaches.

Now self-awareness is self-affirming, self-believing, self-loving. Thus since self-awareness is awareness *in* the total mystery of being and carries a sense of dependence on that mystery, self-love in this self-aware being accentuates the above-named note of dependence. That is, it is a state of *trust*. We trust life, and not to trust life is to sink into a pathology: and even from such a pathology, trust can never be entirely absent.

Self-love trusting in the mystery that embraces me is that essential act of living that we call desire. Desire, whereby alone a person lives, is the trusting relationship that binds the person to all being, becoming actual. Desire is "stretching" in the reality I am in.

This relational context of desire is vital to our understanding of desire. We have only to reflect on the family likeness between the concepts of desire and hope, and between hope and trust, to get the point. Desire is hopefulness and trustfulness: and hopefulness is hopefulness *of,* trustfulness is trustfulness *in*. In other words desire is embedded in a relationship, what Marcel called the nuptial bond with life—which he found wanting in the thought of Sartre.

When I want something very much, when I feel my future to be invested in some relationship in the most inclusive sense of that word relationship, what is happening is that the relationship that I am with the mystery of being is becoming alive and inviting. Desire is love trying to happen. Always the mystery is prior and all-embracing. In the heightened consciousness of the mystic, the all-embracing mystery is known as the spouse, its drawing the subtle ruses of the lover in the Song of Songs. For the mystic is someone for whom the logic of desire is explicit and a consuming passion—the logic that is most clearly seen in the desire to know coming up against the fact that the answer to the question, Why is there anything? envelops one in its incomprehensible mystery. The more one has experienced this enveloping, the more one comes to think of desire as invitation from the incomprehensible mystery which seems to take the initiative, and the language of that wonderful biblical erotic poem is found to be about far more than sexual love or—what comes to the same thing—about sexual love in its ultimate meaning. Rabbi Akiba, the remaker of Judaism after the trauma of its break with its Christian progeny, called the Song of Songs the holiest book of the Bible, "the holy of holies." And according to a story in the Talmud, he was the only rabbi to see God in this life and survive. Shorthand: the only teacher who saw God and survived got sex straight!

Once we understand desire—all desire—as solicitation by the mystery we are in, we understand something that is often noted in spiritual writings: that whereas desire that is simply a felt need ceases once the need is satisfied, vital desire *increases* with satisfaction. C. S. Lewis says, of what he calls the sweet desire, that the one thing one longs for once the desire has gone is to have it again, to be once again aching with it. This increase of desire with fulfillment, of course, is only intelligible once we understand desire as a trustful relationship. One can always be more trustful, more connected, which means more desirous.

However, the statement that vital desire grows with its fulfillment does not adequately distinguish it from a phenomenon with which we are only too familiar: the more I get, of money, power, consuming, the more I want. The differentiating thing about personal desire is that it *desires* its own increase, as does the desire to know—I don't merely find myself wanting still more *once I've got what I wanted.* The lustful and the power-hungry do not *want* to want more.

Still, there are desires that cease once they are satisfied—the desire to be warmed and fed for instance. Where do they fit into a philosophy of desire? Well, for a start, we have to resist the tendency, legitimized by Freud, to understand all desire on the pattern of these basic hungers. But I think we can go further, and understand the basic hungers in the light of vital desire. We can stand Freud on his head. It is surely significant that the only three proto-myths that Northrop Frye finds to be absolutely universal are: of the meal as a communion with the divinity, of sexual union as such a communion, and of our life as a journey. In other words, food, sex, and death, the three points where our life is consciously animal, are sublated, in the universal consciousness of humankind, into consciousness as dialogue with ultimate mystery. So to understand our basic hungers in terms of our eternal hunger is to go with the flow of all our psychic energy.

Now if my trusting relationship with the mystery is what desire actuates, the enormous changes that that relationship undergoes will mean corresponding changes in desire. And since these changes in the person-mystery relationship are precisely the growth crises of our life, these crises will bring about changes in desire. Between the desire of the infant for the glory of maternal embrace and the desire of a Gandhi to restore the self-love of a people, and, at the limit, the desire of Jesus for a baptism that will send fire through the earth, there lie many growth crises. The process is one of desire coming ever more into its own, coming ever closer to being the actualizing of that relatedness to ultimate reality that the person is. It is the liberation of desire. Eventually we shall be seeing desire liberated in Jesus, in a death in love, with his followers awakened to this state on encountering him in his glory or fullness of divine life.

What changes, I have said, is the way in which I feel situated in the total mystery. We must now look at this situating, to see whether we can find in it a structure in terms of which successive transformations may be described.

Just before we go on, however, a precision may be useful. People say to me, "You are talking about a certain *kind* of desire, aren't you?" I want to answer, "No, I am trying to talk about that of which all desires are kinds." It's a sort of concrete universal, I think.

3

The Structure of Growth

Human infancy is shaped by two pulls: the oceanic pull of the womb, and, in tension with this, the growing sense of being separate. Oneness and separateness are in a tension that will exist until our death. In this tension, out of it, the ego forms. I think of the pearl forming in the oyster shell through the interaction of the shell with the tender flesh. I am using the word ego much more loosely than Freud, to mean any sense of myself as individual.

But the ego of childhood is only a first form of ego. With it established, the original tension will reassert itself and demand a fuller resolution. In adolescence, the pull of oneness will be felt again, with new and bewildering force, in the form of sexual passion, and a new ego-form will have to be arrived at.

In the course of life, a person who continues to grow will have to go through many such reassertions of the tension. The crises of life, whether of falling in love, undergoing conversion, suffering bereavement, or a host of other eventualities, all present the painful and bewildering demand that the person die to the existing ego-form and into a new interaction of the two great constitutive forces, of oneness and separateness. The person dies into a fuller selfhood, that is to say, a recon-

15

ciliation, at a deeper level, of "being myself and no one else" with "being one with the pervading mystery." The pneumatic or spiritual breakthrough that became Israel is an enormous advance in this direction. For it is the discovery of personal freedom (from all the cosmic forces, the gods) *in* oneness with the transcendent whole.

Now we have to be more specific about this forming of ego out of the tension of oneness and separateness. It is not to be conceived of as a compromise between the oceanic bliss and the harsh reality of finite existence. The whole idea of life as a compromise, as a coming-to-terms with a harsh reality, as a reconciling of contradictories as best one can, is the negative heritage of Freud and many other makers of the modern mind.

In reality, the oceanic feeling and the feeling of separateness are mutually advancing. A person in love was never more him- or herself, never more absorbed by the all-embracing mystery of being alive.

This mutual enhancing of oneness and separateness is desire. For desire is, as we have seen, the allure of the whole felt as the life of the individual. It is the relatedness I am, happening. And it wants to happen at deeper and deeper levels, as the creative tension of oneness with separateness seeks ever deeper levels to happen at.

Now this progressive deepening of the creative tension of oneness with separateness is what is happening through the progressive growth crises of our life. A new kind of desire will be only partially understood in the way of thinking that I am leaving behind. I shall understand that I want this or that object. But I shall not understand the new reality, the new interaction of what I call me with strange new feelings. I try to love this person in the old way, and it doesn't work. D. H. Lawrence says of his Christ awakening sexually, "He was absorbed and enmeshed with new sensations." One of the puzzles of falling in love is that desire is not only fastening on a new object (this I understand) but finding a new subject (but who am I?). Intrinsic to the excitement of "you" is a new "me." The new "me" is trying to form out of a new experience of the tension between the oceanic and the finite. In the experience of falling in love, a person senses the real ground of selfhood, which is not "this solid me" but the dynamic interplay of the two forces supporting the ego rather as a ball is supported by the jets of a fountain. How often counseling sessions bog down because the client is unable to say what he or she wants, the clarification of desire being contingent on the emergence of a new self. "Who am I?" and "What do I want?"—these questions exist in a dialectic that is in the nature of growing selfhood. It can be most frustrating.

Thus the growth of a person is the progressive liberation of desire. It is the process whereby desire finds ever more deeply its subject, whereby desire comes to be in one who can say, ever more deeply and wholly, "I want." This process comes from the first cry of infant desire to the final liberation of desire in union with God. We move from the oceanic unknowing bliss to oneness with the *mare pacifico* ("tranquil sea"), as Catherine of Siena calls the Godhead. Desire is fully liberated when a person comes to the deepest self, where identity is at one with the God in whom we "live and move and have our being."

This notion of desire in search of a subject as well as drawn by an object fits into the mystical tradition. The practice of imageless prayer is a clear instance of the deliberately starved mind giving permission to the oceanic to set up a deeper dialogue with one's separateness. Contemplative prayer, like falling in love and once described by Abbot Chapman as "an idiotic state," is desire opening "at both ends"—toward an object, and toward being a subject in a way not yet understood. I do not know who I am with the alluring unknown. The liberation of desire is not "getting what I want" but "coming to want as ultimately as I am."

The whole practice of psychoanalysis can find its ratio in this notion. For psychoanalysis, whether Freudian or Jungian, consists in giving permission for desire, as I do not yet know I have it and that parades before me in the at first incomprehensible form of dreams, to become mine. Dream analysis opens up "this end," the subject end, of desire. And of course Jung's concept of the self as distinct from the ego refers to the ultimate intentionality of the process, to the who emerging from the progressive liberation of desire, to the who becoming able to say "I."

I have long been persuaded that desire is not an emptiness needing to be filled but a fullness needing to be in relation. Desire is love trying to happen. I have based a whole course in theology on this premise. I can now formulate it much more satisfactorily. Desire does not spring from a sense of emptiness, it is true. But there is in it a sense of incompleteness. As I experience it, it is still in the process of *becoming* desire, it is still finding its subject. It is still getting a "who." (And desire wanting to become itself is the same thing as desire wanting its own increase, of which I have spoken.) And thus the notion of a person as a relatedness—which gave Augustine his breakthrough on the Trinity—becomes more deeply rooted. The desire whereby I am drawn to another is partly constitutive of who I am. To be drawn to another is to become more myself.

Robert Doran once said to me that the aim of the Exercises of Ignatius is the overcoming of fear through the liberation of desire. I think this profound comment is elucidated by the way I now understand desire. Fear is *of* the changing of ego that the progressive unfolding of desire brings about. We fear the unknown. Especially we fear becoming someone we do not as yet know. To liberate the desire for this becoming is to come into the perfect love that casts out fear. I have discerned in myself—and have found others in agreement—the curious fact that I dread *not needing* the things I now think I can't live without, more than I dread *actually losing* those things. Any takers? If you agree here, you have an excellent example of our fear of spiritual growth—a fear stronger than the fear of deprivation. Who really wants to feel like Jesus?

The development of desire is a progressive changing of what is desired and who is desiring. That which demands and shapes this changing is the trust-relationship with the mystery in which we live, of which I spoke earlier. The need to change and grow is the need of this dialogue to deepen. The need for this process to come to a full transformation stems from the ultimacy of the mystery that initiates it. For the finite to become one with the infinite is a total transformation. This is what I said at the beginning. Human identity is in the mystery that we call God. We become who we are to the extent that this mystery is working on us, changing us. And perhaps we are at a watershed in Western culture, when the self as isolated monad is breaking down, the self-in-mystery revealing itself as who we actually are.

That which changes, with each growth crisis, is the way in which the abiding tension between the oceanic and the sense of separateness is being currently lived, in other words my present ego, who I am now behaving as though I were. The growth crisis is a bewildering shift in this balance, demanding renegotiation.

But this raises a crucial question. If it is the mystery, "It," that prods me with a call for new attention and change, and if what demands readjustment is a fresh eruption of the oceanic, are the "It" and the oceanic the same thing? A lot will depend on getting clear about this.

Let us recall the baseline: desire as trust in life's mystery, underlying all that we do for good or ill. Now the eruption of the oceanic—whether as adolescence or bereavement or war—is a severe challenge to this trust. It is when the mystery appears thoroughly untrustworthy, capricious, and cruel. And it is precisely this impossible behavior on its part that tells me—tells the prelinguistic center whence, God knows how, we do change—that the existing trust-relationship, the current "deal," doesn't work anymore, and that only when I become somehow different can trust be restored. Disaster challenges me to re-personalize. (Dr. Zhivago, wandering down a country lane wondering how to deal with two incompatible sexual commitments, is seized by a small Red Army contingent and put to work with their wounded for the ensuing years. The incident is integral to the depth of faith in Pasternak's book.)

Thus the oceanic is the mystery felt as dark, challenging our trust in it to deepen. I still remember Augustine's description of the loss of a young friend in death: "My heart was black with grief." The growth crisis is not undergone unless we seem to be swallowed up by the oceanic. How this is not our destruction but on the contrary the threshold of our destined life, is the most mysterious thing in the finite's dialogue with the infinite. It is the experience of rebirth out of death. Sometimes, a friend of mine once said, God wears the soul pretty thin.

And it *is* out of death that we come into our destined life. Death here is more than metaphorical—or if it is metaphorical, we are at the origin of the metaphor. It is not simply the necessity of dumping an old way of being to come into a new, that dictates the description of the old as having to die. It is the death-dealing nature of the whole in which we become ourselves, bringing us to a death that is the condition of our development. All this will come to a focus in those men and women for whom Jesus brought trust in the mystery to within sight of its goal ("Consider the lilies of the field!"), on whom the onslaught of his crucifixion therefore represented all the negative potential of the mystery for the growing soul, who came out of this death into the fullness of desire on seeing him and finding his tomb empty.

Vernon Gregson has powerfully expressed this relationship between the darkness of our world and the development of trust. He says—I quote freely—"Only when we have attained to sacrificial love will the world be one in which God is good—and even then there will be the little children."

Once we begin to understand all conscious life as based on a generic faith or trust in reality, the Bible begins to look quite different. We begin to sense in it the dialogue that life is, in the diverse moods through which the dialogue necessarily passes. In the Psalms there is no contradiction between God as the theme of ecstatic praise and the God who deserts, destroys, forgets his people. It is simply the contrast between trust at peace and trust on severe trial. The Psalms are a challenge to *recognize* the negative moods in our trust that are an inalienable part of a lived trust, one that is not kept in a separate pious compartment but that tries itself on all that is happening in us and to us and around us—tries

itself and sometimes comes up with a blank. Hopkins
has this memorable reflection:

> Wert thou my enemy, O thou my friend,
> How wouldst thou worse, I wonder, than thou dost,
> Defeat, thwart me?

It is impossible to deal with the growth crises of desire
without thinking about death—for death is what we are
talking about when we describe the swallowing up by the
mystery that characterizes a severe crisis. Let us never
forget that the incomprehensibility of God, which can
be experienced philosophically with pleasure, can be for
the mystic the darkest of nights, and for the bereaved
lover death in the soul. It is quite erroneous to think that
we do not experience death until we die. If we have lived
at all, we already know it well. And our *memory* of having
come into fuller life through it should affect the way we
think about our certain final death. And if a person's
growth is a progressive liberation of desire, and if the
person's life moves inexorably toward death, then it
would seem natural to regard death as the climax of this
process. For something in us sees in death a cessation of
our confinement to the space-time continuum, so we
could put together this idea of deconfinement and the
idea of a climax of liberation, a climactic growth crisis.
The liberation of desire would then be the *meaning* of
the ending of our space-time confinement.

May it not be that *insofar as* my consciousness is
shaped by real desire, which is myself wanting to grow, I
see death as this liberating movement, and *insofar as* my
consciousness is shaped by the negative "Freudian" understanding of desire, I see death as the final instance of
that equilibrium which everyone, on this supposition, is
in search of? Part of me thinks:

Into another intensity
For a further union, a deeper communion
Through the dark cold and the empty desolation,
The wave cry, the wind cry, the vast waters
Of the petrel and the porpoise. In my end is my beginning.

And part of me thinks:

Darkling I listen; and for many a time
I have been half in love with easeful Death,
Called him soft names in many a mused rhyme,
To take into the air my quiet breath.

There is the Eliot in us and there is the Keats in us.

This hypothesis does seem to account for the highly ambiguous look that death has for us. Does not all our literature oscillate between death as end and death as passage? And does not our century of mass death instill an image of death as end rather than one of death as passage. "What passing bells for those who die like cattle?" as Wilfred Owen puts it. How fascinating that line is, "cattle" clearly chosen to rhyme with the following "battle," and uncannily right.

And if the sense of death as passage loses its power, the ultimate significance of the liberation of desire throughout our life must come into question. Quite simply, is there any point in wanting to be good? That is Iris Murdoch's question, asked in novel after novel.

So we have to ask: Is there any way in which the sense of death as climactic liberation might prevail in our experience over its negative parasite? Is there any way in which the human journey into divine union through the climactic moment of death might be shown to us, through our somehow dying now, and knowing now the abundant life that comes out of death? This, I shall argue, is what took place for those destroyed by the final crisis of Jesus and brought to life by its sequel. I shall argue that they *knew* the risen Jesus in the liberation of desire, for which the necessary condition was that unique state of annihilation to which the death of that awakener of desire brought them.

4

The Sin of the World

The reader will, I am sure, have felt a certain unreality in the picture of human life so far proposed. Is spiritual growth, with its progression of ego-deaths, happening out there or in here? A psychologist friend said to me recently, "We people in the psychology business tend to come up with general theories about what's going on in people's lives. But we predicate our theories on the people we treat. And people who go into therapy suffer from an excess of humanity! The vast majority of people are quite unaware that they are being manipulative and exploitative." Yes, it is certainly naive to assume that people (we) normally meet life's challenges and grow, that marriages deepen, that societies seek reconciliation and healing.

Now, it is not enough to say that people tend not to grow. It is very important to offer a reason for this, other than negligence or perversity. Christian tradition has a name for the spiritual inertia that is woven into the human condition over and above personal sin: *original sin*. And there is a psychological theory gaining ground today that does come close to describing *psychologically* the condition that we know *theologically* as original sin. What this theory is describing is a systemic societal repression in people of the "true self": the true self that does trust life, that does want to grow, that does "desire to desire more," in other words the self as I have been talking about it. Such a psychological theory, if valid, will help us to understand why the desire to grow in desire, though in the deepest sense normative, is not the empirical norm.

The theory I refer to is that of Alice Miller. In her three books, *For Your Own Good, The Drama of the Gifted Child,* and *Thou Shalt Not Be Aware: Society's Betrayal of the Child,* she lays bare the following dynamic. The infant needs to see himself or herself in the mother. The ego, we have seen, is the balance between oneness and separateness. The infant is drawn into oneness with the mother through seeing *itself* in the mother, and this fascination is held in balance by the growing sense of its separate existence. It is important to understand that this balance is not a compromise. The sense of separateness allows the infant to enjoy himself in the mother-mirror without getting lost in it—to enjoy *himself* there. Now if the mother won't let him *be* separate but holds him to her *as a mirror to herself,* then he is not free to enjoy himself in her. Thus he learns to crush the self in which he should delight, to crush it not only in himself but in the people he meets in later life. Aristotle's insight, that love for another is based on ordered love of self, appears here in a negative form. The prime disorder in self-love is the repression of the self in the name of a parent-identity that the child cannot afford to be without, and this disorder infects all the person's relationships. The brilliant insight of Alice Miller is that what the client sees in the analyst is not the parent but the child he or she has to repress. She has a strong claim to have laid bare our worst vice, the *libido dominandi* ("impulse to dominate"), in its origins. We do unto others what, long before we could do anything about it, was done unto us. I call this "the leaden rule"—it questions the golden rule rather as Hopkins' "leaden echo" questions the "golden echo." We are the prisoners of our parenting far more profoundly than we realize. Miller tells the story of a woman client, a very intelligent person, who, just as the therapy was beginning to work, took to telephoning her in the small hours of the morning to report on her dreams. Together they discovered that the root of this unreasonable behavior was that when she was a little girl her father, an actor, on returning from a performance early in the morning not ready for sleep, used to wake her up and make her entertain him.

The insights of family therapy are vital here. The mistake has been to consider the child by himself, whether as child or in later life. So we talk of the child's unsatisfied narcissistic need. What we failed to see is the effect of this impoverishment in terms of the family, namely, that the child, being weak in ego-consciousness, spontaneously feels like the glue or cement that has to hold the family together. It is this identity with the whole, socially imposed on his or her weakness, that can alienate him from himself for the rest of his life. Studies have shown that the children of alcoholic parents assume compensatory roles in the family. One will become the joker, one the reconciler, one the mascot, etc. The novels of William Goldman, especially *The Color of Light*, throw a devastating light on this phenomenon.

But why is the child deprived of sufficient narcissistic satisfaction? According to Miller, it happens because having a child reminds the mother—and father—of her own partially unsatisfied mirror need in childhood, so that she sees in the child the mirror to herself. As a result the child's vital impulse to see and enjoy himself in the mother-mirror is made to feel shame, because his "real" duty appears to be that of fulfilling mother's expectations. This may be the origin of shame, a quality as fundamental as it is ignored by psychology.

The result is that we do not enter fully into the mirror phase, the first ego phase. Now, this is crucial. *Because we do not enter into it fully, we are reluctant to go beyond it.* It is difficult to leave the house that one is still trying to build. So we spend our lives, in part, taking care of an ego that did not get off to a sufficiently rambunctious start. Of course some people are luckier than others. But society as a whole, with its enormous interdependence and dependence on past generations, will surely reflect this arrest, through insecurity, at the early ego stage. Certainly our society does, and massively. The whole world of the mass media, especially in advertising, is a systematic perpetuation of the infant mirror phase, inviting us to identify ourselves by the right car, the right clothes, the right people, the right body contours, the right cosmetics, the right scotch. We are surrounded with a forest of what a friend of mine calls identity posts. Christopher Lasch's book *The Minimal Self* is a very profound socio-cultural analysis along these lines.

In pointing so searchingly and poignantly to a system of deprivation that, by definition, goes back from generation to generation, Miller has offered a psychoanalytic parable of original sin, and a more potent one than the Oedipal parable of Freud. We are locked into a permanence of early ego, using others as mirror to ourselves, doing to others in the subtlest ways what was done to us in our beginning by parents who had it done to them. "It was a dark and stormy night."

This permanence of early ego, which tends to be the social norm, can obviously take many forms. The constant factor is that basic childhood needs—for attention and for seeing oneself in the mirror of others—*are still being supplied*. The house out of which one should be moving on life's journey is still being built, splendid extensions built on. What is properly regarded as the steering wheel comes to be the compass. When people say that the problem with politics is ego, what they mean is not that there is something the matter with ego, without which we could not survive. They are referring to ego-still-having-to-be-built-up. And it is ego as compulsively self-securing that makes the long journey of transformation to seem quite unreal. This is what I shall be referring to as arrest at the early ego phase. It is an imperviousness to what life is really about, and as such deserves the name of sin.

Once we have built in the Miller factor in all its tragic intensity—with an eye to a pessimistic view that "90 percent of families are dysfunctional"—we shall see that the effect of Jesus on his disciples and on the church that they will become is *not only* the transforming of our finitude by the infinite but also the reversing of a millennially inherited *resistance* to this transformation. We shall be able to understand anew, in terms of our psychological self-knowledge, the age-old insight that our salvation has two dimensions, that of transforming and that of healing. As we shall see, the healing dimension of the Resurrection is forgiveness of the disciples for letting him down, while the transformation dimension is their understanding why he had to let *them* down namely to bring them to the fullness of ego-death that the final transformation involves.

We have outlined a theory of the human condition, in its normative trust toward transformation into the infinite, and in the massive inhibition of this thrust through familial and societal repression of its subject, the true self. What the Christian fact does to this condition is (*a*) to reveal the end and meaning of human transformation by effecting it in Jesus for his disciples, (*b*) thus to restore the transformative dimension to its normative status after it has been virtually eclipsed by sin, and (*c*) to swallow up sin in transformation.

5

Jesus and the Structure of Growth

If consciousness is normatively a progressive dialogue with the infinite mystery in which we are conscious, of which the end is total transformation into the mystery, we should expect this overwhelming fact not to remain in the shadows of our experience as the hope of the wise, but to come upon us with the force of revelation. We should expect the mystery to become as evident (to faith of course, to the open soul) as it is decisive. And in fact all the great world religions look back to a theopany that totally changed life. One of the ironies of much contemporary Christian theology—and, by a double irony, especially of theology shaped too much by scriptural exegesis—is that it downplays the Resurrection, thus depriving *this* world religion of its initial theophany, and thus, by a third irony, weakening Christianity's unique contribution to the dialogue of religions.

The heart of Christianity is Jesus dying to ego and revealing the fullness of life out of this death. This raises a question. We are accustomed to connect the death-entailment of spiritual growth with sin, equating dying to ego with dying to sin. How then can we speak of Jesus, who is believed to have been sinless, as having to undergo this kind of death? The short answer is that dying to ego is not the same as dying to sin. It is the

31

dying to present ego-consciousness, a kind of consciousness that is indispensable but comes to a point
where growth demands that we move beyond it, *at which
point* sin tries to keep it in place. So dying to ego is dying
to sin's anchorage, sin's pretext that one is only human.
The fully liberated human being is one in whom the
death to ego, undeterred by sin, proceeds with far more
vigor. The sinless person dies to ego a great deal more
totally than we sinful people do.

Of course the reason why we equate dying to ego with
Paul's dying to sin is that we are so habituated to our
transformative thrust being kept back by inherited and
ubiquitous sin, that we think of the latter's removal as
releasing the thrust, not realizing that the transformative thrust makes *its own* ascetic demands because
transformation is painful. A person who is lame will
tend to think that, the lameness cured, nothing stands
between him and athletic prowess. In point of fact, an
arduous training awaits him, that has nothing to do with
the cure of lameness.

The only author I know who has made this distinction
between transformation and the overcoming of sin is
Herbert McCabe, O.P. In *God Matters,* he shows how we
have shriveled the Christian message of transformation
of the finite by the infinite to an obsession with ourselves
as "miserable sinners." Then, almost as an afterthought,
he adds, "Of course, being miserable sinners doesn't
help!" That is a beautiful restoration of the classical
balance of the Christian message.

The difference between sin and the reluctance we
experience in face of a challenge to grow is that sin
systematically prevents the challenge from presenting
itself. Sin idolizes the ego at its present stage of development, whether of the individual or of the whole society,
and declares this to be the reality of things. It does this

for the individual: The way I have come to see myself and be comfortable with myself—my tastes, my preferences in friends, my sense of gender identity—that is who I am, period. It does it for society: The homogeneity, the like-with-like, of a class, a race, a gender, in which there is nothing wrong per se, gets absolutized into elitism, racism, sexism, and the like.

Further, what is being absolutized is the repression of self-love, the radical self-negation that sin is. It is not only the ease, the comfortableness of settled ego-forms, that attaches us to them. It is a deeper decision against life, a connivance with the message of early childhood that simply being myself doesn't do, makes trouble. Ironically, it is the choice of what is *not* really comfortable. Martin Luther King, Jr., in prison wrote to his white liberal supporters a letter that still burns the eyes. They had been telling him he was going too fast, and he replied that when black children asked their mommies, "Why can't we eat in that restaurant?" the mother looked away, so that a certain self-disgust was instilled for the sake of survival. And there is evil, said King, and we must end it now. The worst thing about this kind of evil is that you can't pin it down. It's not *in* the parent, or *in* the child. It's not *in* the oppressor or *in* the oppressed. It is not anybody's. Being essentially a depersonalizing force, it is impersonal, a clammy all-pervading climate. And thus the traffic between sin in the individual and sin in society is two-way and easy. We are still only beginning to learn how true this is, to outgrow a spiritual "I'm all right Jack!" that makes us okay the way we are, in our enclaves whose walls grow higher and higher, reflected in the stark housing contrasts in our cities.

This state of an insecure and so tenaciously maintained weddedness to the early ego phase is not the

same thing as the fear that I properly feel when addressed by the transforming power that calls for ego's
dying. It is not the same thing as the fear that Pascal felt
at the infinite wastes of the night sky. Not only is it not
the same thing. The more strongly I experience this
tiedness to present ego, the less I can experience the real
fear of what draws me beyond ego. It is a crucial mistake
to define our fundamental attitude to the infinite by our
insecure attachment to the present ego phase, in other
words, by sin. Our fundamental attitude to the infinite is
defined rather by the chasm between finite and infinite,
and by the awesomeness of the transformation involved
in crossing it. We see this attitude "in the pure state" in
Jesus. It is to become wholly ours. Finitude, creaturehood, is not sin. The fear that the creature feels at
the call to transformation is not sin. Sin is the *absence* of
that fear. Hence the progression indicated in the famous hymn: " 'Twas grace that taught my heart to fear,
and grace my fear relieved." The fear of the Lord is the
beginning of wisdom.

There is an important difference between that fear of
the unknown which is characteristically and beautifully
human, and saying that the known is enough. The latter
is the pervasive sin of the world, the denial of desire, the
ratio of what Lonergan calls the longer cycle of decline,
the arrogance of common sense. It is the opposition to
change in a family, a class, a nation, a race, a gender
group. *Underlying it,* assuredly, is the fear of the unknown, of the love into which we are being drawn. But

to the extent that that fear is recognized, change becomes possible. Thus the explosive confrontations of the
racial drama of the sixties in the South mark the beginning of change—as does the crucifixion of Jesus. A
really sinful situation is without fear, except in the unconscious. It is characterized by a huge complacency, a

triumphant assertion of the status quo that is unaware of its vulgarity and banality. Some find it epitomized in the shopping mall. Thus when the Women of Canterbury confess that they fear "the fire in the thatch, the fist in the tavern, the push into the canal/Less than we fear the love of God," that is the beginning of conversion. Sorrow for sin, when sin is seen as insensitivity to the transforming love, is shame not guilt. Guilt does not reach the perspective of transformation, and there is no mention of it in the Exercises of Ignatius, which speak often of shame. And one thinks of the Confessions of Augustine, read by shallow minds as guilt-ridden whereas it is a celebration of healing shame. Guilt is awareness of sin as attachment to the ego, but is still within the perspective of the ego.

I have been very impressed recently by a statement of a friend of mine, a mystic, who is making a study of the great Servant Songs in Isaiah. She wanted to get beyond either "claiming" the songs for Christianity or "claiming" them for Judaism as spoken in the name of the Jewish people. The meaning of the songs is that the love instilled by the infinite in the finite, and the transformation process into which that love invites, must entail much suffering. I would say that being sinless exposed Jesus to this suffering with unique intensity. This is not the suffering caused by sin. "Oh, yes it is!" it is answered, "it is the suffering caused by *our* sin." And thus, at the crucial point, the insight is missed, and Muddle, that ready ally of religious thinking, reigns. The muddle is to associate *all* suffering, suffering as such, with sin, and to hold onto this connection even in the case of Jesus by the subterfuge of saying that he suffers *our* sin. The truth is that suffering inheres in finitude in the presence of the infinite, and that Jesus undergoes *this* suffering which we, because of sin, are *unable* to undergo until we

see our true self and its proper suffering in him, until
we are back on the authentic human track, having left
the city of the abiding ego. The main point here is that
the concept of the liberation of desire, supremely ap-
plicable to the life of Jesus, shows that unique life as the
magnet that draws us into its trajectory from birth into
eternal birth, instead of leaving us neutral, passive to a
savior the precise nature of whose saving act is, on account of this neutrality, bound to lack the intelligibility it needs to have if we are to appropriate it.
Jesus, sufferer of the infinite, suffers empathically with
that in us which, because of sin, is unable to suffer and it
is the awareness of being suffered-with where sin prevents us from suffering that causes sin to fall away. Sin
deadens the nerve of creaturehood. Being suffered-
with awakens that nerve to pain, so that the deadening
of sin is dissolved. What Dostoyevski's Raskolnikov experienced in the love of Sonya was not something opposed
to his sin, but his sin's undermining by that Christlike
undergoing of the suffering he made himself incapable
of so as to murder the old woman. His moment of
rebirth was when, after he had confessed the murder to
Sonya, she said, "What have you done to yourself?" The
ego made absolute enough to murder puts the real self
beyond the reach of the suffering that transforms—
until another suffers in our presence this forgotten pain
of ourselves. We have to be led beyond the suffering we
bring on ourselves through holding on to present ego,
to suffering the liberation of desire. This, as I hope to
show, was the suffering undergone by the disciples of
Jesus. At the end of a brief discipleship, he imposed on
them a transformative suffering hideous in its incomprehensibility that turned out to be the beatifying
incomprehensibility of God.

Jesus, sinless, is the sufferer of the pain that our ego-fixatedness prevents us from suffering. He is the human being who suffers only God. In his baptism we see him undergoing ritually the death of ego into fuller life, of which Golgotha and Easter will be the consummation. In his baptism, where he sheds the ego of a good Jewish youth for a world-embracing self, we see conversion, not from sin but from innocence, and we see this as the real conversion to which we are called, beyond ego, which is not sin, into a Spirit-transformed life. There is no excuse for confusing "that which has to die" in us with sin, when we have seen it die in Jesus who is sinless. There is no excuse for confusing the creature's reluctance for transformation with sin, when we have seen that reluctance take the form of "dismay" in the Garden, with the urgent prayer that the chalice be taken away. In Jesus we see death to the ego unimpeded by sin but certainly not unattended with dread. Of course it was the appalling pain that he dreaded. But far more, it was the abandonment by his Father, the death component of his final transformation, the descent into hell.

To describe the life of Jesus as one that continually died to ego and into fuller life is not to describe a private spiritual quest, but the direct opposite. By dying to ego, a person becomes progressively more in solidarity with others and alive to the nerve of pain, desire, and hope, that runs through us all. The life of Jesus carries this principle to a new level. His was the suffering inherent in living out the self's true being, which is being-in-oneness, in a way that questions all the defensive barriers between people, all the role-based relationships, that institutionalize the normality and permanence of ego as a way of being. Hence the table friendship with disreputable people; the seeing of women as equals,

unheard of in his time; the relativizing of the Law; the
unmasking of all forms of self-righteousness; the unpre-
dictable behavior of the leading characters in the parables; the wild exaggerations of the Sermon on the
Mount; the image of the grain of wheat dying applied to
himself. The continuous dissolving of ego in its divine
ground that underlies all this unconventional behavior
is the suffering inherent in being human, and that suffering alone. It is creative, transformative suffering.
And it creates the scenario for that rejection by society
that brings him to the cross. To suffer God, to live
exposed as finite to the infinite, to embody the demands
of full humanity, is to court suffering at the hands of a
society loath to leave its defensive citadels. Rosemary
Haughton, in *The Re-creation of Eve*, has some very
strong statements about the violence drawn from people
by insisting on relating to them only as person to person.
Jesus' style of interrelating, simple to state, its apocalyptic in practice, and hastens history to a stark conclusion.
The crucifixion is the expression of his love for people,
not in the loose sense that since he loved people he was
presumably giving his life for them—and "presumably"
gives the show away. The crucifixion was the expression
of Jesus' solidarity with people in that it was the result of
that solidarity, it was that solidarity brought to its logical
conclusion.

And it is only now that I see the reason for my
impatience, down the years, with all talk of Jesus dying
for love. I don't think we really knew what we meant
when we talked this way. Love and death combine too
easily in our romantic soul. In place of this romantic
image of the Crucified, we need the image whose hard
focus is history: the crucifixion the brutal resultant of a
life in solidarity, not for the interpretation of the pious.
Just examine your pain at watching that white woman

journalist, in the recent film *A World Apart,* being pulled out of her pleasant world and brutalized by the police, and realize how glad you are it isn't you, and you are having an insight into Jesus "suffering for love." An English scholar was quoted to me recently as saying that one does not see anything leading to crucifixion in the saintly life of Jesus. An advanced case of scholarly dyslexia. On the cross is the lover of men and women— paying for it. One of the greatest ironies of all is that theologians debated endlessly about the "price" bit of what the human being in all of us recognizes as "the price he had to pay for living that way." To whom was "the price" paid? to God? to the Devil?—much nearer the mark, nearer the original colloquial sense of "the price he had to pay." For who, do we suppose, made it to be the kind of world in which the appropriate reward of love is crucifixion?

6

Jesus and His Disciples: A Unique Intimacy

The next step is twofold: into the experience of Jesus, and into the experiencing of him by his intimates out of which comes the Gospel proclamation. What we shall be studying is the creative suffering-for that Jesus undergoes, in its primary being-for-others, that is, for his disciples.

With regard to Jesus himself, dare we suggest that our proposed structure of the human being standing between oneness and separateness can help us to understand the psychology of Jesus as the God-Man? Let me get at this indirectly. I have recently become convinced that we have to understand the Incarnation in the context of the essentially enigmatic character of the human person. We cannot think of human nature as a simple given, like any other animal nature, as a reality that we essentially understand, and then think of this reality as somehow subsumed (assumed is the traditional word) by the divine person of the Word. It is rather that something essentially opaque in the human—to do of course with being a consciousness between oneness and separateness—becomes luminous, so that we feel, "This is what God was about when he made our strange species and the whole universe that comes to consciousness in

41

this species. This in effect is God's word made manifest, no longer opaquely, as in us, but luminously."

Let us go into more detail. I suggested that the "opacity" of the human "has to do with" the in-between character of consciousness. "To do with" is deliberately vague. Does not the opacity arise, not from the in-between-ness itself but from what we do with it, the virtually universal tendency to interpret our being-in-mystery in terms of our separateness? Indeed it is difficult to think of this ever being wholly avoided, because you can't talk about the mystery side of us except obliquely, and we are inveterate talkers. This confusion may lie at the root of all evil—and did not Becker, a nonbeliever, say that the root of all evil was our denial of creaturehood, our denial of participation in the mystery? Could the psychology of Jesus be one in which this confusion was not made, in which the oneness with the divine ground was lived but never translated into the order of privilege that pertains to the world of thing and language? This interpretation fits in with an understanding of the great kenosis hymn in Philippians 2, that is gaining ground among scholars. It runs that Jesus "being in the form of God *(as all humans are)* did not translate this into being for himself (as all humans do) but on the contrary took our humanness on in an extraordinary way, its true way, a way of total self-dispossession, of freedom from ego, in which (upsetting all our ideas of what befits divinity) he made manifest the ultimate mystery that itself is poor, for-all, has no possessions, makes rank meaningless, which fact became fully manifest in Jesus raised from the dead and receiving the name beyond names." That is pretty free, but I think it a fair paraphrase.

Now this approach enables me to talk much more satisfactorily about the *effect* Jesus must have had on his disciples. I mean, that "sinlessness," which I have made extensive use of in earlier attempts to wrestle with these things, is that very unsatisfying thing, a double negative. A double negative makes a positive, but only in a logical way. What is the concrete positive that was Jesus? What was it that brought our deepest desire out of hiding? This, after all, is what this book is about. "Sinlessness" does not get it, does not suggest what sinlessness lets through. This is the Jesus-effect, loosening in the hearts of his followers a deep closedness to our authentic being and its journey, the silt of countless generations.

The point about Jesus is not that he was sinless, just as the point about transformation is not the taking away of sin. Is it perhaps that sin exploits a certain *incompleteness* in my sense of the mystery as the ground of being, that only time, only a lifetime indeed, will remedy, so that in the incompleteness, in the radical uncertainty, sin makes its short-circuiting bid for divinity. This essential undecidedness looks like Rahner's very creative interpretation of "concupiscence." It is not sin. Can we think of this incompleteness in Jesus as somehow filled with the Spirit which keeps it free for God's progressive self-revelation, as not having the *unfreedom* (for that is what it is) to bid for instant divinity? Sin is the avoidance of our freedom. I don't want to go further into this. And I don't need to. For all I want to show is that Jesus must have had an overwhelming effect on his disciples. If the mystery of Jesus is more than I have said, then the effect is so much more, and that plays in my direction. I would like to "fix" this important suggestion in some stanzas. (I am finding these days that the stanzaic form enables me to say some things more clearly.)

> I live within a mystery,
> Its silence such, there's nothing there,

And our relatedness is such
As speaks to me only in prayer.

What friend ever demanded such
Or showed such patience? There is none.
This friend nothing particular,
Shows no concern at what is done.

Yet of this mystery alone
I have it that I am desire
And that the universe is mine
To bring to light with the mind's fire.

So I live with divinity
As energy of mind and will,
And only patience stands between
Me and the impulse for a kill

That takes the world for me, its god,
Using the light that it denies
And changing everything I see
Into a shimmering world of lies.

And was there one who lived within
The mystery that lives in me,
In the uncertainty that's man,
And yet mysteriously free?

Such a one would be free indeed:
It is unfreedom, desperate,
That grabs at our divinity
And upon meaning cannot wait.

And did the Holy Spirit keep
The future present for his heart
To grow in wisdom patiently
And is this not the Spirit's art?

Tamely we say "he had no sin":
No saying no, and this betrays
How cautiously we speak of one
Who is the essence of our praise.

Before I pursue this question of the impact of Jesus, a
short digression is necessary. For the faith made explicit

at Nicea, Jesus is "one in being with the Father." I have worked through much confusion on this issue, eventually coming to realize that this was due to an unavowed persistence of Harnack's notion of the hellenization of dogma, the notion of a gulf, unbridgeable and not needing to be bridged, between the Jesus of history and the Christ of faith. Once this fiction has been exposed, we realize that the Jesus who in the Resurrection revealed himself as "the Lord"—a revelation that Nicea did not inflate but only expressed in a new Greek word—had to be from the beginning of his life with us "God from God, light from light." So we have to ask ourselves what would have been the impact of *this person* on those whom he called into discipleship. Let this impact be never so unthematized conceptually, it was still the impact of one who was all that Nicea later affirmed him to be. I fear that much contemporary Christology is ante-Nicene (which means, since Nicea, anti-Nicene), preferring to remain within the parameters of "proclamation" and short of an absolute truth-claim for Jesus, and this of course removes all the pressure for my question about the original Jesus-impact, my question being not, What was the impact of Jesus? but, What was the impact of one whom divine faith now makes known to us as one in being with the Father? A much more searching question.

There is a vicious circle in the way we moderns think about Jesus. The Enlightenment's separation between the (unknowable) Jesus of history and the Christ of faith removes from consideration the effect of Jesus on his disciples. And since the church's belief stems *from* this effect, from this first experience, ignoring it deprives the church's belief of its foundation and makes of it a subsequently elaborated myth, which is what the Enlightenment started by assuming. Thus the argument is

circular. The immediate effect of Jesus is unknowable
because there is an uncrossable divide between the Jesus
of history and the Christ of faith. And there is an uncrossable divide between the Jesus of history and the
Christ of faith because the immediate effect of Jesus is
unknowable. What breaks the circle is a third term:
besides the Jesus of history and the Christ of faith, there
is the Jesus who gave rise to faith, the *historical Christ*,
proclaimed out of the encounter with the risen Jesus
and the finding of the empty tomb. "Jesus becoming
Lord and Christ" is a well-documented historical event.
Another way of making the point is to say that making
the divinity of Jesus *depend* on Hellenism conceals a quite
other move: making it *independent* of the first, Jewish
experiencing of Jesus by his disciples.

There is, I think, a transcendental connection between the divine identity of Jesus and the Gospel emphasis, unique in the history of religion, on discipleship.
Since the meaning of Jesus lay in who he was, the
communication of that meaning was primarily through
the "I-thou" channel, whereby person becomes known
to person in the awakening of personhood. It was thus
that Jesus communicated, rather than through the spoken word—and not at all through the written word. José
Comblin, in *Jesus of Nazareth* (Orbis, 1982), says that
Jesus had few very original ideas, the outstanding one
being his own peculiar version of the Kingdom. "They
cited it in the gospels and they attributed it to Jesus, only
because Jesus used it. They did not use it, simply because they themselves did not know precisely what he
meant. It did not serve them in expressing their experience of Christ" (pp. 132–33). The almost invariably
misunderstood saying of Klausner, that "Jesus preached
the Kingdom, and Paul preached Christ," becomes luminous when we understand that the preaching was not

the essential mediation between Jesus and people: when we understand the sense in which Jesus was the substance of his own teaching as well as of Paul's. It was himself, the self of humankind grounded in God and seeking life in God alone, that he presented to a surprised world. In my terms, it was the self uniquely free in oneness, that people experienced without realizing it.

A person for whom the oneness dimension was not tacit and unacknowledged, but lived in and acclaimed intimately as Abba, dear Father, would have awoken in his intimates, men and woman, a self that they never knew they had, yet who they knew they were meant to be. In the old days we used to talk about "the sacred humanity." That term, transposed out of its cozy little conceptualist box into the real world, becomes evocative and exact. To be in touch with sacred humanity was to feel humanity as sacred, the prism of infinite light— which it is, but very confusedly, as I have argued. The effect of this presence was to awaken desire in its original intention. As Françoise Dolto, that little-known French octogenarian Freudian, splendidly says, *"Jésus enseigne le désir, et y entraine. Jesus entraine au désir, et non à une morale."* ("Jesus teaches desire and draws us into it, into desire and not into a morality.") In the disciples of Jesus, what Alice Miller, another liberated Freudian, calls the true self is awakened—and is thus able, in a bewildering crisis that still haunts the memory, to be denied.

The Gospel narrative lays the greatest emphasis on the psychological crisis that the crucifixion was for the disciples. The crisis is presaged by their uncomfortable feeling that Jesus is wedded to his oncoming ordeal, and this horrifies them. The weddedness is not masochistic. Jesus is not attracted to the cross. The cross is attracted to Jesus, as the consummation of a death in love with all,

as the destiny of the man of oneness in a broken world.
And the narrative is at pains to show that this was quite
unmanageable by the disciples. Peter's violent protest at
Caesarea Philippi and Jesus' violent response indicate
this. And the theme of scandal is a leitmotiv of the
narrative, reaching a high intensity at the end. "You will
all be scandalized in me" could be paraphrased, "You'll all
wish you had never known me." Peter's protest on this
occasion meets with a rebuff in harmony with the one at
Caesarea Philippi: "You? You'll be the worst casualty of all.
You'll deny you ever knew me!" A friend who, it turned
out, had been researching the same material with the
different purpose of developing a theological base for
bereavement counseling, has suggested that Peter's denial
was prompted not by mere fear but by rage, the confused
rage of someone lifted to the heights and dropped into
chaos. And the final desperate cry from the cross was
recorded, though it told against pious intentions, because
the seeming abandonment, of him and so of them, by
God, was remembered as an essential moment in the
process of whose outcome the Gospel is the celebration.

We now have to carry through the disciples' involve-
ment to its final stage, their response to the end of Jesus.
First of all—I now think—they participate in it by being
agents in it. In the end, there were only two sides to be
on, two positions: the world, and Jesus. All crises of this
kind show this final painful narrowing of the options as
the crisis is upon us.

If I may be allowed a short excursus on my history of
dealing with this dark mystery of our salvation: in my
first serious attempt, *The Crucified Jesus Is No Stranger,* I
saw the whole thing centering around *our agency* in the
crucifixion: it means us destroying our true self. Then I
came to see the centrality of the disciples, the intimates
of Jesus, and what, as his intimates, *they* underwent at

the end. Now at last I see that *both* are central. The disciples both brought on and suffered the end of Jesus. They have let him down and been let down by him. They have done what we all do, gone along with, let themselves be carried along by, the general consensus of the half-alive against the fully alive, the socially legitimated downing of our greatness, our true self. Through the contagion of Jesus, the true self was very much alive in them, so they were killing it in themselves in a far more suicidal way than were the other people. It is the unimaginable and worst of all possible betrayals, as when Winston, in *1984,* to save himself from "the worst thing in the world," blurts out, "Do it to Julia!" In other words, the whole human evasion of transforming union, sin with the biggest possible *S,* is brought into sizzling contact with what is evaded, the self now awakened, the self now in love, the self now in sight of its grail. This, I now suggest, is how our life-evasive life was taken into the true ego-shedding life in its moment of final climax and thus, in a psychological dead land never entered before, was able to receive the revelation of him in his final glory as who we are and who we are to be. Making a rather more direct use of the oneness-separateness idea for my class, I have suggested that being intimate with Jesus, the man of oneness, enabled them to experience the oneness we are thrown into with death, while being held in the balance of this life by his companionship— which, removed, flung them into death in life. And recalling what I said earlier, it seems that their letting down of him, their self-denying, pertains to the healing dimension of the mystery, his letting down of them to the transforming dimension.

This is how those men and women have known, *in this life,* that final growth crisis which, enigmatically withheld from us on the other side of death, leaves us only half-believers in our journey into God, half-committed to the liberating of desire. May we not see the Jesus event as a telescoping of time, a drawing up of endless time into simultaneity? The Spirit-filled life of Jesus, as we have seen, brings into a supernaturally patient growing the inconclusive dialogue in us between self and mystery. The inconclusiveness of the dialogue puts its resolution on the other side of death, whereas with Jesus the resolution is now and death is its manifestation, so that it brings *them* into the now this side of death. *Ipsius sunt tempora et saecula* ("his are the times and the ages"), said in blessing the Paschal candle, is no mere rhetorical flourish. It comes out of an experience of the eternal in time, the experience of those who followed Jesus all the way beyond the grave.

I think Schillebeeckx, in *Jesus*, considers only the disciples' letting down of Jesus, not his letting down of them, so that their being forgiven this, which certainly is central to the encounter with the risen Jesus, is not presented by him *in its enormous context* (which is the realization of why he had let them down), namely, the "life-giving Spirit" bringing eternal life out of the horribly scenarioed death of ego.

And I have to remind myself that if this talk about oneness and separateness in elucidation of the Jesus mystery seems outlandish, we moderns find outlandish our own deepest rooting in oneness, out of which virtually all the historic descriptions by the human of the human come to us. When everyone stops knowing what they know, it is difficult to start them up again.

7

<hr>

The Transformative Liberation of Desire

What we are tracing is the story of a radical transformation, of the people in a community, as a community. In order to do this, it has been necessary to know what transformation is, what is the structure of this process. We have seen that the growth crisis consists in the breakdown of the existing ego-form, the person's present way of finding his or her sense of oneness within the sense of separateness. What the New Testament presents us with is the growth crisis that precipitates that radical transformation, that meaning and end of all transformations, which is union with God, or, as the Greek Fathers call it, apotheosis, deification.

What brought the resolution was the Resurrection. But for this assertion to have any meaning, a lot of spelling out is required. A vast amount of scholarship has been devoted to studying the New Testament documenting of the Resurrection, and the research continues unabated. For a taste of the complexity of the matter, one has only to work through Pheme Perkins's fine study *Resurrection.* The reason for the complexity is that very little in the texts can be taken as straight reporting. All the accounts of meeting the risen Jesus bear the marks of sophisticated editing. Our texts come to us from ages before the concept of straight reporting, or of scientific history, arose. A report would be edited in order to bring out some aspect that the writer thought especially important from the point of view of his particular theology. Luke's Gospel, to counter the views going around that Jesus was not a real person but a mere appearance (a view commonly followed in practice though not of course in theory) has Jesus explain, "A ghost does not have hands and feet as you see I have."

Two main elements, in a complex of stories and sayings, are clearly discernible: the discovery of the tomb empty and the appearances of Jesus.

The first element: The women, to their complete bewilderment bordering on panic, find the tomb empty. One thing is very clear as we probe the text, and it is of crucial importance. The tomb being empty did not mean, to those who discovered it, that Jesus was risen. On the contrary, it was the occasion for nothing but surprise and shock. It is only a resurrection reduced by Christian habit to our space-time dimension that makes of the empty tomb something not bewildering but obvious. The angels by the tomb are surely part of the editing, to set the empty tomb *in the completed kerygma.*

The second element: Various people, singly and in groups, are said to have "seen" him. The way in which this is generally put is, that he "appeared" to them.

The real question is, How did the first community *connect* these two elements? After years of thinking about this whole affair, this is really beginning to look to me like the essential question. We have got so used to their connectedness, that we miss the original bewilderment that is of its essence. "He left the tomb and showed himself to people," is the way we package it.

The original connecting might have gone like this. The tomb is discovered empty by the women, to their consternation and fear. Angels at the tomb announcing the Resurrection are a later addition. Then there are the encounters with Jesus, which have a transforming effect, bringing the devastation caused by the crucifixion into a new sense of utter security and peace and joy, drawing into this new unity the tangle of emotions— shame, guilt, fear, anger—released by the fate of Jesus. We might call this the "positive" Resurrection experience, the empty tomb the "problematic" Resurrection experience. This is the peace and joy of a death of ego brought to its transformative conclusion. The ego- death, the emotional chaos into which the disciples have been thrown, finds its meaning, and they are alive as never before.

What does the empty tomb do for one who has met Jesus risen? Here is a suggestion. In a mystical rapture, in which our space-time limits are dissolved and eternity is tasted, something in the unconscious of the experiencing animal says, "Perhaps I am dreaming." It is not noticed. It is not avowed. It is a natural kick of the animal in us. What the sight of the empty tomb does is to bring this skeptical reaction to consciousness *and refute it!* The order of the eternal and the temporal order are brought into contact, which only accentuates the discontinuity between them. And of this discontinuity the empty tomb, the sheer absence it bespeaks, is the sign. The point is that the new presentness of Jesus as joy, forgiveness, liberation, is *in another order,* is another order supervening, than the order where tombs and corpses belong. We have got so used to putting them into the same order and deriving the nature of that order from the empirical realm of tombs and corpses (and in consequence emptying out the essence of Resurrection faith) that we have constantly to remind ourselves that, no, the New Testament witness clearly has two orders here, two sorts of reality, the first characterized by a discovery at a tomb, the second characterized by shared spiritual transformation. It is the

second of these that dictates what is going on, and that
gives a strange resonance to the first, making it mean,
"It's him all right that we are encountering, but extraordinarily, in a way that takes us beyond ourselves into a
new world."

The amazing discovery that the tomb was empty must
have delivered an extraordinary message to the psyche
destroyed by the end of Jesus and woken to new life by
the encounter with Jesus risen. I suggest that this message was that the death of ego, the inner annihilation
they had experienced, extended to death itself, to the
sheer physical fact that broods over all our myths of
rebirth; so that they now stood, as a community, where
none had stood before, in the world after death, known
heretofore by speculation alone. This was the experience that grounded "realized eschatology," Paul's con-
fident assertion, "You have died, and your life is hidden
with Christ in God."

And *then* (the last thing to dawn on them) the image
of the empty tomb suggests that the transformative experience they are now having is the beginning of the last
age, "when the tombs shall be opened, the dead rise,"
the apocalyptic event thus symbolized strangely pre-
viewed in the disappearance of the body of Jesus from
the tomb. Very strangely indeed. The final resurrection
is still symbolic of another order. The empty tomb is still
empirical, in this order. It is not a question of "OK, so
it's begun, starting with Jesus." The transformative
nature of the experience remains the controlling factor,
keeping the mind focused on the felt presentness of
Jesus, with the empty tomb sounding its peculiar note of
realism. This total, engulfing reality that has taken hold
of us has left a sign of itself in the common world. The
empty tomb shows us that there is no way back for us
into the common world the way it was before he turned
it upside down. And the austere balance of the mystery,

keeping the integrity of the symbolic and of the empirical and not confusing the two, while calling forth faith as the balancing point, allows the mystery to speak to a later, more epistemologically fastidious age.

Instead of the empty tomb giving to the encounters with Jesus their meaning, which would be simply "he's alive," a prosaic meaning void of the overwhelming sense of transformation that is their essence, the encounters and the growing experience of the new community in the Spirit give to the empty tomb *its* meaning which, far from being prosaic, is a total break with the prosaic, a turning of this world into bewilderment. We are now in a world where corpses disappear! I would say that if the appearances of Jesus are thought of as removing the surprisingness of the empty tomb ("Oh, I see why he's not there. He's come to life, and left the tomb.") the whole message of the Resurrection has been missed.

On this showing, the discovery of the tomb empty, which we see and liturgically interpret as the dawn of Easter, was originally experienced as *taking even further* the confusion caused by the crucifixion. The Emmaus story suggests this. The two disciples tell the stranger the story of the last few days, and end by saying, And now—"to make matters worse" is the sense—some women are telling us they found the tomb empty (Luke 24:21).

Finally, if the empty tomb discovery was originally part of the bewilderment caused by the end of Jesus, then we can see that this was how the women suffered the confusing break with all expectations, whereas the men suffered this more "politically," in a world of men, as betrayal, denial, flight. The men fell flat on their faces. The women, patient and attentive to the immemorial decencies of life—going to anoint the body—suffered the shock of the new in their own way.

When I came out to the United States in 1971, it was commonly being said in theological circles that the empty tomb is a latecomer to the kerygma, a pious legend to illustrate the Resurrection faith. I do not know how widely held this view is today, but Gerald O'Collins, S. J., in *Jesus Risen* (Paulist Press, 1987) lists thirty "recent and contemporary exegetes and theologians who defend the essential reliability of the empty tomb story" (p. 123), and Pheme Perkins, in *Resurrection* (Doubleday, 1984), makes the point that the inventors of a pious legend would not have made women its main actors, since the testimony of women was not accepted as valid in those days (p. 94). She shows that neither can the empty tomb tradition have produced the appearances tradition, nor the latter the former, and concludes with what every Christian knows: "However, the combination of an early tradition of appearances of the Lord and the conviction that Jesus' tomb was empty would help to explain the significance of resurrection in the Christian message about Jesus" (p. 84).

A thing that has hit me only recently is that the dismissal of the empty tomb wipes out the witness of the women. And the mischievous thought follows on this, that this may be a piece of unnoticed spiritualistic male chauvinism. The Resurrection is a "spiritual" reality. It has nothing to do with corpses and tombs—the sort of thing the women were concerned with.

What has given the empty tomb story a bad name is that it has been understood as the *continuity point* between the death and the resurrection, thus reducing the Resurrection to the purely empirical level of the crucifixion. In fact, the empty tomb is the opposite of this. It makes visible the *discontinuity* between our world in which Jesus is crucified and the world to come of which he is the center and the life. It seems to me that the story of the empty tomb is integral to the story of transformation that is the life and liturgy of our faith. Rowan Williams, in his *Resurrection* (Darton Longman and Todd, 1982), refers to "an echo of bewilderment, shock and disorientation which we have noted in our stories. The risen one, the exalted one, addresses the community from *outside* . . . And for all four Gospels, the story which identifies the ultimate source of this disorientation is that of the empty tomb" (p. 105). So much for the idea, often met with today, that the empty tomb makes belief too easy.

If Jesus "lived in the mystery" in a dialogue that was not intermittent and inconclusive but growing in the Spirit, then death for him was not that on the other side of which alone resolution could come. Rather, it was the completion of a resolution never in doubt. Most importantly, this meant that the death of Jesus was homogeneous with the death he died every day. So that the disciples, made to suffer this death and knowing its consummating sequel, were able to embrace, in the death of ego, or daily dying, the death that lies ahead of us. Life is no longer lived under the shadow of death, it is in the light with death behind us. The virus of eternity has entered our bloodstream for ever. Of this fact the church is the always defective but sure sign.

Physical death is no longer "something else" than our dying to ego, but is anticipated by it. And really to believe in Jesus, to be in love with him, that is, to allow his death to be in us as death to ego, is to live with death behind us. So Paul can say, "You are dead, and your life is hidden with Christ in God" (Col. 3:3). The whole Pauline doctrine of baptism as being dead and buried with Christ begins to look different, to have deep psychological roots, to refer to undergoing with Christ that liberation of desire which death expedites.

So it looks as though "Dying, you destroyed our death" misses it—he did not destroy our death. He restored it! He made it work. He took it out of the bushes along the way, stuck it right up in front of us, and took us through it.

> Dying, your brought us to death:
> Risen, you are our life.

The events of our story fall into the form known as a chiasm. In its simplest form, it is the rhyme pattern *a b b a*. "I used to think/That people knew/When I feel blue/My spirits sink." The great chiasm goes like this. There is the life of the disciples with Jesus beyond this world, the ministry, the "Galilean springtime," as Renan romantically calls it *(a)*. Then, in brutal contrast, there is the shockingly worldly event of the crucifixion *(b)*. Then comes a further shock, the empty tomb *(b)*. Finally there is the perfection of life beyond this world, with the risen one in the Spirit *(a)*. The revelation has a wonderful aesthetic coherence, which gives it great power.

What Christian faith, and it alone, affirms, is the deification of man by God, in the person of a man who is God. This work of the Holy Spirit is the liberation of desire. Significantly, the Holy Spirit dilates the heart and enlightens, these two as one. And so the liberation of desire is identically of heart and mind. Desire liberated is the desire to look upon the face of the beloved, the desire to know, which knows nothing of that split between mind and heart of which our culture is dying.

A more personal note: The death of Jesus has always had for me a beauty that is the beauty of myself directly expressed, to have the richness of the reality most beautiful to me, namely my own. I used to love it when it came to Passiontide with its magisterial opening, *Christus assistens pontifex futurorum bonorum* ("Christ the High Priest of the good things to come"), and the moment in the church in the Roman Campagna with the canons singing atrociously, "one of the soldiers opened his side with a spear." And I could never get this sweetness into words, could never get any further with it in words. It is coming back again these days, recalling the sweetness of those earlier days.

I am sure I am nearer to its formulation now, in saying that that death is my own—and therefore all the world's—transformation into God, and that it can be that because it is physical death expressive of the death of ego, which only that death is, because of Jesus' absorption in God throughout his life, an absorption that his death would enact.

I remember being electrified by a very long book by Maurice de la Taille, S. J., called *Mysterium Fidei,* for de la Taille saw Jesus at the Last Supper not just *signifying* his sacrifice but *making* it. I was very frustrated when a fine theologian told me de la Taille was all wrong, that he made too much of the ritual aspect. Jesus gave himself up in death, not at the supper table. It was a moral, not a ritual sacrifice. Exactly as would be the death of any martyr or mother or self-sacrificing soldier. In this insistence on the moral against the ritual, the unique mystical electrifying enormously mysterious meaning of Christ's death was lost without the man even seeing he was losing it. It is extraordinary how good people manage to trample sapphires into the mud without noticing it.

I do not need the ritual category today to *explain* what I mean about that death. Today the ritualizability of that death flows out of its inherent quality as physical death expressive of the death of ego. It is by that inherent quality that it speaks to me today as *my own* becoming who I really am in God.

My own and everybody else's. For the self that I touch here is at once the most private and the most universal reality. It is the word in my flesh leaping to the word made flesh.

St. John was surely working out of the same intuition when he heard Jesus as saying to the people, "I lay down my life of myself, no one takes it from me. I lay it down, and take it up again." I die as I live whose living is the unhampered, unconfused dying of ego.

This is how that death, the *beata passio*, belongs for me with C. S. Lewis' "longing that pierces you like a rapier with the smell of a bonfire," the reminder of a self that is of God.

> Desire to see the face of the beloved
> Is the desire to know, bears us beyond
> All that we know we are or know to covet,
> The very reason why the heart is fond.
>
> Jesus teaches desire, and draws us there
> So that we grow, and do not know ourselves
> Knowing ourselves for the first time as prayer
> Descends us to the deeper ocean shelves.
>
> All anger at untruth lost in compassion,
> We learn the truth whose reign is in the heart,
> The split of mind from heart after world fashion
> Mending at last under the Spirit's art.
>
> Jesus the liberator of desire
> Once seen in heaven, is the heart on fire.

PART TWO

Implications

8

For a Proper Resurrection Realism

A recent book, *Did Jesus Rise from the Dead?*, by Gary Habermas and Antony Flew (Harper and Row, 1987), makes one realize what a gulf now separates the Scripture scholars from the average intelligent believer, and the following observations aim at suggesting a bridge.

The substance of the book is a debate between Gary Habermas, of Liberty University, in Lynchburg, Virginia, and Antony Flew, the well-known British atheistic philosopher. Flew goes in first, and he begins by "spelling out three fundamentals upon which Dr. Habermas and I are agreed, notwithstanding that many of those still claiming the Christian name will, nowadays, make so bold as to deny one, or two, or all of these fundamentals. First, we both construe *resurrection* in a thoroughly literal and physical way" (p. 3). The other two points are the centrality of the Resurrection, and the Godhead of Christ. He goes on to say, "David Jenkins, a man who has repudiated, and still repudiates, the doctrine of the Resurrection, and that in words too offensive for me to repeat in the presence of genuine believers, was elevated to the senior bishopric of the Church of England."

The first thing that strikes one about this is the gulf that separates Flew's way of talking from the world of discourse of Scripture scholars of whatever stamp. And

63

yet their way of talking has about it an ambiguity, a
reluctance to raise certain questions of truth, that is as
unsatisfactory in its way as the feisty language of Flew.
Somehow the two worlds have to touch: Flew's intol-
erance of ambiguity needs to find a language consonant
with the profoundly mysterious nature of the Resurrection, and the scholars' language needs to shed a *kind* of
ambiguity that evidences epistemological confusion
rather than awe at the *mysterium tremendum et fascinans*.

First, then, the Resurrection of Jesus is a unique
event. It does not belong to a larger category called
"resurrection." It is the voice of God in history bringing
history proleptically to its end. It imposes the same
condition of "knowing unknowing" as does the Godhead itself. We do not know what the Resurrection is, as
we do not know what God is. And yet we know it, and we
know that through it everything is changed. The same
goes for our knowing of God, as I suggested in my first
chapter.

This means that we cannot lay down rules that the
Resurrection would have to conform to to *be* a resurrection. We cannot, for instance, require the disappearance
of the body. Suppose for instance that the body had
been dissolved in quicklime as used to be done with
hanged persons—and Jesus *was* a "criminal"—would the
Resurrection have been impossible? The idea is absurd.
So we cannot say that resurrection involves something
happening to the corpse—what if the corpse were no
longer existent? To modify the rule to run "The corpse,
if there, would have to be dissolved," would be imperti-
nent and humourless. It's the remark of the student in
the class who still hasn't got the point.

If definition and resulting rules are out, how are we
to proceed in this vital matter of understanding the
Resurrection? Not surprisingly, we have to concentrate
on *the way the Resurrection became known*. In other words,

how was it originally presented to the bewildered understanding? How did the revelation of the mystery happen? As long as this is the question, as long as what we are investigating is the actual becoming known of the Resurrection (and not, "what *is* a resurrection when it's at home?") the answer is not in doubt. The Resurrection became known through a conjunction of "seeing him" (and being totally transformed) with finding the tomb empty. It is on this strange conjunction that we must concentrate.

The notion that the empty tomb tradition is late and legendary is now more and more rejected. It is a canard. And the view that it was legendary has a concealed "must" in it. It must have been legendary, although it is in all four Gospels and the whole Easter story falls to pieces without it, and although the Christian Sunday is probably commemorative of finding the tomb empty on "the first day of the week," and although the rejection of its historicity wipes out the witness of the women, *because* the Resurrection, properly understood, does not involve the disappearance of the body. Who's making rules now?

The more I look at it, the more the empty tomb appears to be, not a materialist debasement of the mystery, as the Bishop of Durham thinks, but a mysterious concession of the mystery to our way of responding to the fact of death. I mean, however exalted the present state of Jesus, however discontinuous with our mundane habits of mind, a corpse means that the person is dead, and this is incompatible with the statement that Jesus is alive, if that statement is meant to mean more than the statement of a believer in immortality that *all* the dead live on.

And of course it means more. The whole tenor of the Easter story is different from the conviction of a group that their leader "lives on." The difference lies in the grounding of this conviction in two devastating experiences: the seeing of Jesus and the discovery that his tomb is empty.

Between the two poles, of Jesus present and the tomb empty, the mystery addresses us. Any attempt by us to cross that gap, certainly the "obvious" one of saying that Jesus came to life and left the tomb, violates the mystery, the sacred space in which it becomes known. And so does any attempt to dissolve the "material" pole. What God says to us is, "Jesus is not among the dead" (the empty tomb) and "Jesus is eternal life, one with me" (the appearances of Jesus and the coming of the Spirit). It is not for us to join these two poles, except to learn that he who was dead is now life. It is not for us to imagine the transition from the one to the other. St. Thomas says that not only was the Resurrection of Jesus not witnessed, it was not witnessable: "Christ's resurrection . . . transcended the common knowledge of humankind at both extremes: at the starting-point when his soul returned from the underworld and his body from the sealed tomb, and at the term when he attained the life of glory. Therefore, his resurrection should not have taken place in such a way as to be seen by people" (*Summa Theologiae*, III, q. 55, a. 2).

I think the notion of a divine "concession" to history, to us, is a valid one. In the days before the term acquired its present connotations, theologians used to speak of the divine condescension. As mysterious in its way as the mystery itself is the "trace" it leaves on history. History registers it as an upsetting of its regular patterns—not the ridiculous upsetting that Gibbon demanded in his famous ironical passage (How was it that no one in ancient Rome has recorded the darkness that came over the whole Earth when Jesus was crucified?), but a very quiet enigma only perceptible to someone patiently examining the matter, the inability of any "normal" hypothesis as to what might have happened to stand up. The old apologetic that dealt with alternative possibilities—such as that Jesus went into a deep swoon on the cross and revived in the cool tomb, or that the disciples stole the body, or that the women mistook the tomb—does spell out the enigmatic historical deposit of the mystery. Every possible alternative to a wildly improbable story is manifestly implausible! As someone put it to me, "When God enters into an argument with us, he doesn't lose."

Thus I cannot dismiss the rambunctious debate between Flew and Habermas as simply missing the point. What they are arguing about, what Habermas affirms and Flew denies, is really the implausibility of *anything else* having happened, of an alternative at the level of the "historical deposit." They think they are arguing about what did happen, which presents them with no problem as to its description: this perfectly clear and definite thing called Resurrection did happen according to Habermas, did not happen according to Flew. And here of course they are missing the point, and a Scripture scholar sensitive to the richness of the mystery will be rightly put off. But a sense of the richness of the mystery that does not include the problem it sets for one who would brush it aside (or subsume it under Joseph Campbell's splendid array of archetypes) connotes a loss of exegetical grip. What Flew and Habermas are doing is arguing around this problem, this deposit of the mystery in our history.

Gerald O'Collins is surely right in saying that the vast majority of Christians see the empty tomb as essential to the Resurrection—in a way, I would add, that does not distinguish between the mystery and its historical trace or deposit. He cites the recent graffito, "There will be no

Easter this year. They have found the body." The refine-
ment I am suggesting is necessary, I think, if we want a
theology of the Resurrection. But the Resurrection faith
can survive without it. For the common Resurrection
faith is suspended between the two poles, as my account
is. This faith does not consist in picturing Jesus leaving
the tomb—significantly the weakest theme of Christian
painting. It holds that the tomb was empty, and that
Jesus is present, prayed through and prayed to. God
knows his business better than do theologians.

The reason why an orthodox theologian will want to
ask questions about the empty tomb is as follows. What
the Resurrection showed, and shows Jesus to be—"life-
giving Spirit" (1 Cor. 15:45), identical with the all-tran-
scending God—simply is not measured up to by the
statement, "He came to life." Thus when Flew says that
he understands the Resurrection "in a thoroughly physical way," if he means that the Resurrection *is* Jesus
coming to life, something that could be imagined happening, he is not talking about the Resurrection as the
tradition understands it. He is talking about resuscitation. The problem of the empty tomb, for an orthodox
theologian, is not a problem with the vanishing of a
dead body. That would be a problem with miracles, and
that is not a Catholic problem. It's certainly not my
problem. The miraculous has happened, in a crudely
empirical way, to a close friend of mine, and I have a
perpetual novena going to Thérèse of Lisieux. The
problem of the empty tomb for an orthodox theologian,
or better, the task it imposes, is to be clear about not
identifying the Resurrection by what, in our world, happened to the body, but to keep the Resurrection identi-
fied by the glory, the Godhead of Jesus, which is absolutely incommensurate with anything we can conceive of
as happening to a corpse. The miraculous historical

entailment of this self-revelation of Jesus as God incarnate, of the Resurrection, is not itself the Resurrection. It is the ineffable telling us in our language that Jesus is not dead. For Jesus alive we must look elsewhere, to the church (God help us!), to a cosmos in transformation, to the beginning of the end. This lesson has been delivered, with eloquent irony, by history. The cynical Dean Inge commented, on visiting the Holy Sepulcher, scene of warring Christian sects and money grubbing, that it certainly conveys the original message, "He is not here!"

If we believe the tomb was found empty, as Aquinas did, then his belief that the Resurrection itself was unwitnessable forces us to distinguish, as I am doing, between the mystery and its historical deposit. For to believe the tomb was found empty is to believe that the body miraculously disappeared, and an invisible disappearance is sheer nonsense. We have to say that the disappearance of the body was visible—yes, even the famous hypothetical television camera would have picked it up—but that this was not the Resurrection but its "historical deposit."

So, to reiterate, the mystery has two explanatory poles: the transformative experience of the disciples and the discovery that the tomb is empty. Each is necessary to the Gospel's version of how the Resurrection became known. I am happy to have at last got free of the bias that sees only the visionary experience as explanatory. But I would urge very strongly that its importance is not lessened but enhanced by the presence of the other pole. For those who had seen him and been transformed, lifted into the new age, the empty tomb must have been quite devastating. As I suggested in chapter 7, it would have touched a feeling latent in any mystical experience, "perhaps I am dreaming"—latent, not expressed, *until* the fact of the empty tomb *brings it to awareness and denies it.* That meant, "This is for real, all the way. The world is changed, all the way. There is no way back to the way things were."

The people who found the tomb empty, and the people who saw him, were not the same people. The people who saw him did not wonder whether the body was still in the tomb. (Why would they? Would you have?) The people who found the tomb empty did not wonder whether anyone had seen him alive. (The body had gone, that was all.) Thus the two experiences, of finding nothing in the tomb and of seeing him, existed each in its own right. The connection was not of their making. It was utterly mysterious. It *was* the mystery. They had to let themselves be worked upon by it. The connection was not of their making. Working upon them, it was their remaking. Quite bewilderingly at first, they suffered a spiritual awakening that spilled over into the empirical world. They felt myth becoming history. They felt directly the action of the God who joins soul and sense beyond our power to conceive or to undo. If ever a terrible beauty was born, it was then.

In sum, our understanding of the Resurrection is both deepened and clarified if the method we employ is to re-create psychologically the experience of the people who first received it. This means to recover the Resurrection as revelation happening. The empty tomb *told them* that Jesus was not dead. The empty tomb *told them* that they were not "on a high" with the experience of Jesus risen and the Holy Spirit. The empty tomb *for them* did not make things easier but harder, cutting off all retreat from the new age with its absolute demand.

It is when we lose this focus, and imagine the empty tomb as a knock-down proof *for us,* as though our television cameras were presenting it to us, that we get into the problems of the Bishop of Durham with a "laser-beam God."

If they were not deceived, the body vanished,
And that already is to name a question.
"You must not wonder how!" has to be banished
Or God is voodooed: this we cannot rest on.

For common sense, miracle is exception,
Whereas it is revealing of an order
Simpler and yet inclusive, where the depth shone,
Momentary dissolving of a border.

To canonize the world of common sense
Secures a longer cycle of decline,
Setting the ramparts of our self-defense
Whose ancient genius love will undermine.

In that last night of man, a fetus curled,
Another order broke upon the world.

The Question—2

Did you—the question tries to come,
As you begin to open me
Lest I too easily succumb
To a belief that is not free.

Did you—is all this really true
which, if it is, then yes, you did,
And what you did at last comes through:
It is, that you rose from the dead,

And try to make me question you
Out of a doubt I do not know
But you know well, whom torture drew
Inward to where no God can go.

And what if you tore from this flesh
The word of resurrection,
Would it not leave a wound as fresh
As time where the eternal shone?

> The word is yours, the flesh is mine
> Till Spirit blows open my doors
> When I adore you as divine,
> The word is mine, the flesh is yours.

A clarification on method: I submitted this chapter for publication to a leading Catholic periodical. An exacting editorial board came up with the following questions, by addressing which, I think, I clarify what I am saying.

1. What is the Flew-Habermas debate about?
2. What are you reacting to in it?
3. What is the question, exactly, that you are trying to answer?

Habermas and Flew are debating about the Resurrection, Habermas saying it happened, Flew that it did not happen. But what they both *mean* by "the Resurrection"—the meaning they're agreed on—is, "the dead body of Jesus coming to life." Now the dead body of Jesus coming to life is something one can *imagine* happening. And with the great majority of scholars, and with Aquinas, I hold that the Resurrection is not something one can imagine happening. Thus the debate as to whether the body did come to life—as to whether this imaginable event did take place—is not equivalently the debate as to whether the Resurrection happened. This is their debate (first question), and it misses the substance of the Resurrection (second question).

However, it seems highly probable that the encounters with the risen Jesus, in all the circumstances totally transforming in their effect, were startlingly and indeed frighteningly confirmed by the discovery that his tomb was empty. I am suggesting that this discovery should be regarded as speaking to an incredulity that the encounter would naturally provoke—an incredulity to which the record bears witness. It said, to the most earthy part of the psyche awaking to faith, "He's not dead anymore!" It did not, and it could not say, "He's alive," *in that sense in which Christians for two millennia have known him to be alive,* cosmic in his sweep, embracing all times, our saving God in the flesh.

Thus the emptiness of the tomb *confirmed* the faith born of seeing Jesus. It did not, and it does not, tell us how to think about the Resurrection as "a body coming to life." A body coming to life is imaginable, and the Resurrection is strictly unimaginable.

However, the disappearance of the body—quite different from "the body coming to life"—*is* imaginable. An invisible disappearance is sheer nonsense. But this imaginable event is not the Resurrection. According to that excellent and very faith-filled scholar Rowan Williams, the empty tomb comes through our texts as a theme of puzzlement, even consternation. We ought to see the empty tomb as a strange trace left by an ineffable mystery in our empirical world, not as our clue for thinking about, praying, the mystery. The difference between these two positions is the difference between night and day. The empty tomb is a concession of the eternal to the primeval in us.

What has happened, however, is that empty-tomb-centered thinking has filled, quite improperly, the intellectual space that the mystery should occupy. So when the scholars opened up the incomparably wider dimensions of the Resurrection witness, they tended to banish the empty tomb as a materialistic perversion. Instead of demoting it to its proper place, they banished it. "The Resurrection is not the resuscitation of a corpse," was the cry on the lips of popular theologians in the seventies. This is true enough, but easily leads to the *further* statement that the Resurrection has nothing to do with the corpse—which makes mincemeat of the Easter story.

It is not the empty tomb itself, but the empty tomb taken to be the clue to what the Resurrection is, that provoked the Bishop of Durham to say, "I don't believe in a laser-beam God, a God who zaps," which provoked such a furor. Unfortunately he didn't make this distinction, because he is not asking the right question.

This brings me to the third question, which is the heart of the matter, namely, What is the question, exactly, that I am trying to answer?

I think the wrong question is, "What is a resurrection, and what does it entail?" I think the right question is "What *was* the Resurrection, and how did it become known?" If we stick with the first question, we either make the empty tomb to be what people think about, so that they miss what the Resurrection says to the deepest thing in us about the world and us in the world, or we dismiss the empty tomb as derogating from this wider perspective. Flew-Habermas and Bishop of Durham David Jenkins are two sides of the same coin. With the other question, however, the empty tomb is allowed to play its original, real, and unique role in the experience of the disciples who had let Jesus down and been let down by him and then seen him and been filled with the Spirit. Rowan Williams gets this essentially *dramatic* role of the empty tomb in the memorable statement I have already quoted, referring to "an echo of bewilderment, shock and disorientation which we have noted in our stories. The risen one, the exalted one, addresses the community from *outside*. And for all four Gospels, the story which identifies the ultimate source of this disorientation is that of the empty tomb" (*Resurrection*, p. 105). And after all, if the empty tomb is not logically necessary for the Resurrection faith (which liberals say it isn't) then the disciples had no reason to invent it (which liberals say they did)!

A most important thing I have learned from writing this book is that the encountering of Jesus risen is necessarily elusive. Its authenticity demands that it be so. There is a quality of *envelopment* about his presence to them, which cannot be pinned down, and Pheme Perkins emphasizes this. Now this elusiveness, which is the authenticity of the experience, easily degenerates when verbalized into vagueness and uncertainty. That which prevents this is the fact of the empty tomb. This "anchoring" quality of the empty tomb is what is implied in the following statement of Arthur Darby Nock in his classic work, *Early Gentile Christianity and Its Hellenic Background* (Harper Torchbooks, 1962, p. 108): "Yet it must be remembered that in the earliest Gospel record this *third* day rests on an elaborate chronological framework of circumstances which we must regard either as historical or as a complete fabrication. The clearness of our record on this point is in striking contrast with its variations elsewhere." The thoroughgoing fabrication that is the only alternative to an actual memory cannot be seen, with any degree of psychological realism, as combining with the spontaneity of the Easter faith. Thus the two poles of the Easter experience are not the empty tomb and a blinding vision, both of which would be in the same order of miracle. They are the empty tomb and an enveloping re-creative experience, which are not in the same order but, complementing each other and bringing the two orders together, burn the impression of the risen one into the faithful soul.

> We must not ask what resurrection is,
> What the requirements of our definition.
> Rather, what was the Resurrection, his
> To those who knew the failure and derision.

How was it known? First he appeared to them
And they were filled with ecstasy, and doubt
Rose in them at a depth unknown till then.
Pain was in store: they were to have it out:

The tomb was empty. There was nothing there!
Even after the vision, this confused,
Uncomprehending, they could only stare
At truth so obvious that it bemused.

The empty tomb was not to satisfy
Requirements, but to draw faith's painful cry.

9

The Apostolic Witness

In this chapter, I step right outside the area of my competence, into that of New Testament scholarship. I only want to say how struck I have been by a recent possible revolution in that area that speaks very closely to my central concern with the first Christian experience.

All the serious work I have done since *The Crucified Jesus Is No Stranger* focuses upon the effect of Jesus on his disciples. Christianity stems from the transformation of these men and women through a uniquely God-identified life, a correspondingly devastating death, and a final liberating vision whose discontinuity with time shows itself in an empty tomb. All that tradition has subsequently had to say about Jesus comes out of that bloody theophany.

Now if there was this experience, if these men and women knew, with a certainty that is God's illumination of the human mind brought to a climactic intensity, that they had witnessed the end and the beginning, they must have felt impelled to see that their crucial experience would survive in some form. And if the Christian claim for Jesus is true, and not a mythic projection onto an unknown past, if Jesus really was what the Church claims him to have been, then he must have seen to it that he was understood by his disciples sufficiently for their preaching to proclaim *him*. He must have seen to it that they got him right. So there would have to be, doubtless at first orally communicated, copious first-hand reporting of the pre-Resurrection Jesus. To deny any such necessity, and to make the Resurrection a sufficient base for the preaching is to make "the Resurrection" mean no more than the birth of a myth.

Thus if our tradition preserved no such first hand testimony, but only the records of unknown authors in an indefinable relationship with the actors in the original drama, we should have to conclude that no such sense of overwhelming urgency had possessed those actors, and that no such definitive experience as Christianity posits had in fact occurred.

I am not a Scripture scholar, but it seems to me that just such a tenuous first link in the chain is suggested by the almost universally held opinion as to the provenance of our written Gospels. Matthew, we are assured, is not the tax collector, Mark is legendarily connected with Peter, Luke better connected with Paul, who never knew Jesus during his lifetime. And John . . . well, John!

Almost all expositions of the three synoptic gospels take as "a practically certain result of modern study of the synoptic problem"[1] the belief that Mark's Gospel is the earliest we have. The implications of this belief are much more far-reaching than one might suppose. They concern the first Christian experience in its most radical implication, namely the sense the new believers had of now knowing what being Jewish was all about, of their fulfillment as Jews. Of this experience of the *épanouisse-*

---

1. Sir John Hawkins in *Horae Synopticae*, quoted in Bernard Orchard and Harold Riley, *The Order of the Three Synoptics: Why Three Synoptic Gospels?* (Mercer University Press, 1987), p. 3.

ment of Israel, the classic statement is of course Matthew's Gospel. And if that Gospel is the earliest, as tradition unanimously asserts, then what we have in it is the dynamic tension of Jesus with Israel *as experienced by the first generation* of the new believers. The first and vital link of the chain that binds us all to our Jewish beginnings is a *documented* experience of the new.

No such first link exists for those who deny to Matthew the status of first Gospel. For Matthew is then put later, so that its author is not one to whom, desolated by his death, Jesus risen showed himself and who, in the light of that transformative experience, is seeking to understand his Jewishness and where the new community stands in relation to the Law. We are not hearing the people to whom the transforming of history happened telling us about it. And so we do not feel compelled to believe that this total transformation did occur. If they left its documentation to hearsay, how crucial was it for them?

The point, put more briefly, is that if Matthew's Gospel is not the first, there is no apostolic first Gospel. If Mark's Gospel, whose context is the gentile mission, is first, there is no Gospel of the church's first mission, which is Jewish. And it has always seemed to me extraordinary that the first full account given of itself by the Jewish sect that eventually got the name "Christian" should be frequently explaining Jewish customs to pagans, while a later account, derived from the first, takes for granted the hearer's Jewishness and understanding of them. The whole thing seems back-to-front.

Thanks to the painstaking and protracted (in the case of one of them, an English monk, sixty years) labors of a small minority of scholars, we are now able to see that the received account *is* back-to-front. The whole thing is spelled out in *The Order of the Synoptics: Why Three Synop-*

tic Gospels?, by Bernard Orchard (the monk I refer to) and Harold Riley.[2] It is rare to combine the pleasure of a sophisticated whodunnit with the joy of finding strengthened the historical foundations of one's faith. As an example of the pleasure: On the assumption that Matthew and Luke are copying Mark, comparison of the three texts demands that we describe their copying action thus: "At every point where Matthew ceases to follow Mark's order, Luke continues in it. And wherever Luke ceases to follow Mark's order Matthew continues in it (p. 7)." So Matthew and Luke, independently of each other, somehow contrive between them so that whenever one changes the original (Mark's) order the other will keep it! Then the pleasurable insight comes: but suppose Mark is following Matthew and Luke, then when their orders don't agree he perforce chooses one and not the other. You have one man making choices between two others, as opposed to the two independently and alternatively choosing him. When an upholder of Mark's priority (a headmaster of a public school) used the analogy of trying to find out who, of three boys sitting next to each other in an exam, was cheating, Bishop Butler commented, "For a headmaster, he's weak on how boys cheat." This author had Mark as the boy in the middle, flanked and copied by Matthew and Luke. What would have intrigued Bernard Lonergan is that the image he is using contains the answer, but he's getting the wrong answer out of it by failing to keep his eye on the image while considering certain data, namely that Matthew and Luke, who can't see each other's papers, are copying Mark *alternatively*. Once you do this, it springs to the eye that Mark is the copier. Mark is in the middle all right, and he stands appropri-

2. Cited in the previous note.

ately between Matthew and Luke in the canonical order. However, the center is not the source of the two streams but their confluence.

The book contains a great wealth of such insights, rendering the received account more and more gauche. These are developed by Riley in the first part. Mark's Gospel, the shortest and deemed therefore the first, is, pericope for pericope, the longest, combining the accounts of Matthew and Luke.

The reason most people give that Mark could not have had Matthew before him is forcibly expressed by B. H. Streeter: "Only a lunatic would leave out Matthew's account of the Infancy, the Sermon on the Mount, and practically all the parables, in order to get room for purely verbal expansion of what was retained."[3] This reaction, however, ignores what has since come to be a central principle of Gospel criticism, namely that a Gospel is written with a particular community and its particular concerns in mind. The situation that Mark is addressing is dramatically different from Matthew's, as we shall shortly see.

With the ground thus prepared, Orchard gives a very thorough account of the first centuries, during which Matthew's text is cited and echoed well before any of the others. Decades previously, Orchard had shown that it is clearly echoed by both letters to the Thessalonians, which are thought to be the earliest of the Christian Scriptures.[4] That was just fifty years ago, and here we still are with Matthew dated outside the apostolic era. The tradition, Orchard shows, is unanimous that Mat-

3. B. H. Streeter, *The Four Gospels* (London, 1924), p. 158, quoted in Orchard and Riley, p. 79.
4. J. B. Orchard, "Thessalonians and the Synoptic Gospels," *Biblica* 19 (1938).

thew's Gospel, written "in the Jewish style,"[5] came first, that Luke's was addressed to the new gentile churches, and that Mark took down the lectures of Peter in Rome.

The book concludes with a conjectural reconstruction of Peter's lectures in Rome "before Caesar's knights," showing how Peter could have collated the Jewish Gospel of Matthew—which he could have known by heart—with the gentile Gospel of Luke in order to show them as one Gospel, thereby discharging the reconciliatory charism that is central to the Petrine office.

Thus the agony of the birth of the new life out of its Jewish matrix is clearly and strongly reflected in the progression of the Gospels. Not only do they *tell* of our birth in Christ. They *show* it, in dealing with its three stages: of consciousness of new identity (Matthew), of independence (Luke), and of reconciliation of the newborn with the mother (Mark). These are the stages discovered by Margaret Mahler in *The Psychological Birth of the Human Infant*. There is the infant's first sense of being an individual. There is the phase she calls "practising"—exploring, reveling in new skills (which Mahler, rather fascinatingly in our context, calls "being in love with the world"). And there is the phase of "rapprochment" with the mother and consolidation. And then there is Hegel, with his thesis, antithesis, and synthesis. In short, there is life, pulsing before us in these records of our beginning as eternally alive.

When one contrasts all this with the reigning orthodoxy, one has the sense of coming out of a dream. How inept it now seems to regard Mark as the "primitive" Gospel. With all its roughness in style, Mark is a sophisti-

5. This phrase in Papias (c. 60-139) was later mistranslated "in the Jewish tongue" to give rise to the myth of an original Aramaic Matthew.

cated latecomer to a rapidly evolving scene, verging on what we shall find in John. The affinity between John and Mark has often been noted. Mark begins, "The beginning of the gospel of Jesus Christ," a very compact phrase. In Matthew, "the Gospel" is something Jesus preached. In Mark, more theological, it is something that Jesus was and is.

And "Q!" Q—from the German *Quelle* ("source")—is the hypothetical book of the sayings of Jesus whence Matthew and Luke had to get all that they couldn't find in Mark, which was an awful lot. I remember Ronald Knox concluding his review of another important book belonging to the minority report, *The Originality of St Matthew*, by Christopher Butler: ". . . and Q didn't write at all!" One might paraphrase Churchill one more time: Never was so much based by so many on so little. Very recently someone said to me, "Some people are getting worried because there is no mention of the Resurrection in Q." We invent someone who never existed, and expect him to proclaim the transformation of existence!

The received opinion that Mark's is the original Gospel is insensitive to the fact that it was not originally intended to be a Gospel at all, and was not at first recognized as one. Without a beginning or an apotheosis for its hero, it is episodic in form—its rough style matching this—being composed essentially of the *chreiai*, or episodes, recalled by Peter. It is ironic that the eventual, nonprimitive allocation of Mark to the category of Gospel should have misled the critics to the point of having them call it the *original*, the Ur-Evangelium, the pattern Gospel! It's all back-to-front.

It is only when the picture is restored that we realize just how poor we have been with the picture the way it was, the smoke-blackened mass with just a hint of Rembrandt's light coming through. To change the metaphor, it is like having been lame for as long as one can remember and then having the full use of one's limbs restored. And it must not be forgotten that the presuppositions of "the two-source theory"—Mark and Q— were philosophical as well as exegetical. The seemingly simplest and least miracle-laden of the Gospels was preferable for the Enlightenment with its avowed intention of burying the supernatural. "The leaders and heirs of the Enlightenment set out with the deliberate intention of destroying the hold of the Christian religion on the educated classes ostensibly because of its association with the political and spiritual thraldom exercized by the governments of the *ancien régime*" (Orchard and Riley, p. 112). And far more effective than open refutation was this creation of half a century of silence between the Jesus explosion and us, its heirs. We know that silence only now that it broken. We know our lameness only now that it is cured. We know the obscurity of the picture only now that its clarity is restored.

The late Bishop Butler once said to me that the strangest mixture of agnosticism and piety led scholars to withhold from the central figure of the Gospels intelligence and a mind of his own. As though he were too mysterious—meaning, of course, too doubtfully existent—to think! And I am beginning to think that the reason it has taken me decades to see that the unique effect of Jesus on his disciples is the clue to the whole thing—the depth of the plunge, and the radical death-transparenting nature of the sequel—is the agnosticism about the historical Jesus that pervades our scholarship and stems from the Enlightenment. The Enlightenment did some indispensable things. But it also did us out of Jesus, the Jesus the church has known from the beginning.

Finally, let me quote Orchard and Riley's admirable summation of their aim:

> An adequate solution demands reasons not only for the fact that Mark's pericopes are almost always longer and fuller than Matthew's or Luke's, not only for Mark's "zigzagging" between Matthew and Luke, not only for the virtual unanimity of the patristic evidence in favour of the priority of Matthew, but also to explain why there are *just three* Synoptic Gospels, no fewer and no more. And since all theories of Markan Priority rely either on a hypothetical source or questionable conjecture, which all have the effect of dating the Gospels later than the Apostolic Age, there is now warrant for a study that places them a generation earlier, and thus firmly in the historical context of that very age. (p. x)

I feel very encouraged in my attempts at psychological reconstruction of the Christian primal scene by the realization that much of the incredulity that this provokes is due to that obfuscation of Christian origins by the Enlightenment which still affects the climate of New Testament study. It seems unreal to speculate about the psychology of people who are thought to have left us with no strong personal record. It makes a crucial difference to the fortunes of psychological interpretation if the words, "You will all be scandalized in me tonight," are known to express a personal memory. I have heard it said that to understand the difference between a disciple and an apostle, between the stage of being taught and that of being confirmed and sent, one must have died. It seems unrealistic to be exploring psychologically this terribly searching process if we do not have before us the documentation of the apostolic mind that emerged from it. It is of this mind, its Jewishness transformed in Matthew, transcended in Luke, transcendently recovered in Mark, that we have been deprived and must be repossessed. And what are we to make of a Peter lost in history and picked up only in the claims of the Catholic church?

The more we look at this prescribed gap between the event and its documentation, the more we see its ramifications. For once the gap is regarded as a chronological fact, a time interval of two generations, we have to put the Jesus of history on the other side of it, the Christ of faith on this side. And the way from the one to the other is across the minefield of Kant. The combination of the silence of history over the crucial period with the systematic split between the phenomenal and the noumenal has been devastating. Bultmann is its genial emblem. This whole philosophical cast of mind does get one into thinking in terms of a world in which nothing *happens.*

But all things have their time, and the time of the Enlightenment is running out. That is to say, it is revealing its dogmatic presuppositions. The received separation of the Christ of faith from the Jesus of history started as a programmatic decision on the part of Reimarus, "completely to separate what the Apostles present in their writings (i.e., the Gospels) from what Jesus himself actually said and taught during his lifetime."[6]

In reality the difference between the Jesus of history and the Christ of faith is even greater than the Enlightenment supposed. For it is the difference between Jesus crucified and Jesus risen. It arose not in the slow course of time, but in a flash of insight, when they saw him and the tomb was found to be empty.

In the world of Scripture scholarship, the claim for the priority of Matthew is still thought of as analogous to

---

6. Quoted in Orchard and Riley, note 4 to p. 112.

the flat-earth position. That this is no longer the case is indicated by the following, from C. S. Mann in the Anchor Bible (1986):

> On every possible count, Matthew must be regarded as the most fundamentally "Jewish" of the synoptic Gospels, and on this premise alone we are entitled to ask what manner of Jewish Christian community, circle, or individual would find it possible or even desirable to produce our present Matthew at any time after the horrors of A.D. 66–70. We are compelled to reexamine, on the very grounds of its "Jewishness," the whole question of the priority of Matthew raised in acute form by Griesbach. "First the Jew, and then the Greek" would not only do justice to the realities of the missionary situation of the primitive Christian community, but would also do justice to the manifest differences in orientation between Matthew and Luke, for all their similarities in literary respects.

One of the assumptions required to buttress the idea of a late Matthew is, because of its manifest Jewishness, the existence of a Judaizing community in Jerusalem after the total destruction of the Jewish hegemony by the Romans. That is the assumption that Mann finds incredible.

The only problem I have with Orchard and Riley's book is that the picture of Peter running together the accounts of Matthew and Luke is difficult to square with the highly structured nature of Mark's Gospel. A book just published, *A Virgin Called Woman: Essays on New Testament Marian Texts*, by M. Philip Scott, O.C.S.O. (Portlegone, Northern Ireland: Bethlehem Abbey Press), shows that this Gospel is a massive chiasm *(a b b a)*. The incidents in it can be lettered from A to M and back to A', with, plum in the middle *(M)*, the words, "This is my beloved Son: Listen to him!" heard by the apostles at the Transfiguration. But this beautiful discovery only accentuates the main point of Riley and Or-

chard's book: the essentially consequential, late-comer,
harmonizing nature of Mark's Gospel. In spite of its
rough style, it is a very sophisticated arrangement of
preexisting literary materials. Far from being "the most
assured result of modern scholarship," the priority of
Mark is one of its greatest blunders.

> The time has come for us to turn the tide:
> Jesus silenced by the Enlightenment
> Cries out again, leaving his Father's side,
> "How can you worship me, and be content
>
> "To listen to the wise who say that I
> Was a mere flash that came and went again
> Leaving some trace, after a century
> Picked up, and penned in bits as they explain.
>
> "The men and women that I touched with God
> Who died with me, and lived to see my grave
> Empty, does it not seem to you as odd
> For that vision to vanish as a wave?"
>
> We know them well, for they have set it down:
> They are Matthew and Luke, and Mark and John."

10

The Crisis of an Ethic Without Desire: Human Sexuality

The crucifixion of Jesus with its pneumatic sequel is the final liberation of desire into the divine union that all desire is groping toward. But when we ask how these two realities, the saving cross of Jesus and human desire, have been connected historically, we get an amazing answer. First of all, we find in our history a systematic distrust and suppression of desire. Alice Miller's devastating account of this has already been referred to. From generation to generation, "what I feel I want" has been thrust from the child's mind by what Miller calls poisonous pedagogy. And philosophy since Descartes, for all its emancipatory intention, is virtually silent on desire. The amazing thing is that the cross of Jesus has been presented to us not as our liberation from this repressive mind, but as its endorsement! How has it come about?

Basically, there is the misunderstanding of suffering that we have already looked at, the failure to distinguish between the suffering we bring on ourselves by our refusal to grow—by sin, in other words—and the suffering that growth itself entails. Of course they are intertwined, inextricably, but they are nonetheless distinct, and spiritual progress is discernibly the slow prevailing of transformative over ego-centered pain. Failure to observe this distinction makes "bearing the cross" mean bearing the suffering our sins deserve, and although this is called sharing in the suffering of Jesus which is *un*deserved, it is never made clear how our deserved suffering connects with his undeserved suffering. Nor can it be, for if the predominant idea of suffering is as something deserved by our sin as opposed to something inherent in our participation in a transcendence-oriented universe, what is the meaning of undeserved suffering? So suffering with Jesus means undergoing the suffering our sins deserve, with Jesus the sinless sufferer as our model. This hardly makes sense, but the words of the penitent thief suggest themselves here: "We are getting our just deserts, but what evil has he done?" If he who did no wrong accepts this suffering, *how much more* should we sinners accept ours! There is a kind of logic to this, but it does not take us far.

And what does it mean, to suffer what we deserve? It means, to this commonsense way of thinking, to suffer *for following our desires.* Jesus, it is implied, suffers not for following his desires but to fulfill the will of God.

The truth is surely that Jesus does suffer for following his desires. That is what the cross is all about. His desire, totally liberated toward union with God, totally resonant with God's will, draws upon him the vengeance of an unliberated and fearful world. And he draws us to follow him on this *via crucis,* this way of liberated desire in an unliberated world.

Once we see it this way, the sufferers for undenied desire, in their prisons all over the world, the Gandhis, the Kings, the Mandelas, who speak for the desires of the oppressed millions, come out of the Limbo to which a decadent Christianity has consigned them: men and women who have dared to desire. (From what a distance we admire them in movies like *A World Apart!*)

So what we learn from the cross is, not to deny our desires, to push them down, but on the contrary to *attend* to them, to ask of them, What *do* I want? and hence to begin to learn the difference between the compulsive, unfree, addictive movements that go by the name of desire and give desire a bad name, and the élan vital in us of which these movements are the arrest, the dead-ending; the difference between the desire of the ego to stay where it is and simply to repeat past satisfactions, and the desire that can say, "I want to want more," and that alone leads to suffering with Christ. Martin Luther King, Jr., suffered with Christ the desire for his people's dignity in a world that denied it.

What we learn from the cross is the difference between liberation *from* desire (the latter equated with the insatiable self-promoting ego) and liberation *of* desire from the chains of my customary way of being myself. Two contrary views of asceticism present themselves here. The conventional view is that it means denying ourselves things we want. A more discerning and disconcerting view is that it means dropping things we no longer want, admitting to ourselves we no longer want them, and thus giving our journey, our story, a chance to move on—to which our Pauline "old self" puts up a far greater resistance than to more seemingly self-afflicting deprivations that often minister to the ego.

Of course it is difficult to see the cross this way, and seems to be stretching meanings. There's the figure on the cross, naked and abandoned. And there's Paul saying, "Those who belong to Christ have crucified the flesh with its appetites" and "If by the Spirit we have put to death the deeds of the flesh we shall live" and "The

spirit lusts against the flesh, the flesh against the spirit."
And there's *The Imitation of Christ*. In vain do the Scripture scholars tell us that by "the flesh" Paul means our
insatiable egoism that must utterly die if we are to come
out of the half-life that goes for life in normal society.
We know what the flesh is. It is sex. And we know what
the spirit means. It means prayer and so forth. Yet such
an interpretation will not bear examination once we ask,
Did God create sex and say "That's good!" or didn't he?
The idea that one of God's principal prophets is telling
us to choose one half of God's creation and reject the
other half is ludicrous. But still it won't go away, that
naked tortured figure.

And God forbid that it should go away! A therapy I
am using with myself is to switch from Jesus for the time
being, and think about Nelson Mandela and those
twenty-five unrecoverable youthful years spent behind
bars. I ask myself, Does he put me to shame for my
enjoyment of life "while he's in there"? Yes, but this is a
cover story. Really, he puts me to shame for risking so
little. Risk is the refusal to forget desire.

A comment suggests itself, in this connection, on *A
Course in Miracles*. This charismatic, and extraordinarily
prolific, "word" from a contemporary mystic takes the
form of Jesus speaking to us today. The main theme
is that our emphasis on the cross has been a huge mistake, and Jesus apologizes for giving rise to it. And,
apart from this text, how often we meet that phrase "emphasis on the cross," generally used to deplore this
emphasis. Of course what we are running into here is
precisely this ruinous identification of the crucifixion
with the negation of desire, of creativity, of the élan
vital, whereas it is precisely the liberation of these
things into the eternal life that is the heart of the universe. And the identification of the cross with repression

stems from the deeper error of thinking of suffering only from the standpoint of the ego, never from the standpoint of transformation. The moralistic cross is the cross without transformation, without grace, without resurrection.

It is because we do not understand desire but equate it with egoism, that we see the cross of Jesus as opposed to it. Real desire is what the cross empowers, bringing us to the death that its liberation entails. The death is the death of our present ego, whose perpetuation is the work of egoism posing as desire.

Real desire, what I really want and have always wanted, is to be more and more myself in the mystery in which I am. It is the relatedness that I am to everything and everyone in the mystery, trying to realize itself. Desire is love trying to happen. It is the love that permeates all the universe, trying to happen in me. It draws into its fulfilling meaning all the appetites of our physical being. It turns the need for shelter into the sacrament that is a house. It turns the need for food and drink into—well, Babette's Feast! And it turns sexual passion into—ah, there we have a problem. The sentence ends with "marriage," and this is true. But the biggest ethical gap in the Christian tradition is the failure to say anything much as to *how* that taking up of sexual passion into authentic desire, of which marriage is the institutionalizing, happens.

What is authentic sexual desire, celebrated by the Song of Songs and in the first chapters of Genesis? To begin with, it is odd that we have no easy, comfortable common word for it. "Sexual desire" is very stilted. On the other hand, there are plenty of colloquialisms for it, but they all belong to what Renee Haynes once brilliantly called the shadow language. But there is nothing in between, in the world of *"Buon appetito!"* "That's because this is sacred." Oh, give me a break! Anyway, we're stuck with "sexual desire."

No desire is so prone to self-deception, to the very subtlest ploys of our egoism, as is sexual desire. No desire, therefore, is in such need of being understood correctly. But for no desire is this need less met by our Christian tradition.

> Sin, misinterpretation of our godness,
> Raises the spirit high above the flesh,
> Looks with contempt at its resulting oddness:
> So shame is born, and seeks to make redress.
>
> With shame as teacher, we confound confusion
> Asking of what we have to be ashamed.
> Thus we accept as leader an illusion
> And look around for what ought to be blamed.
>
> We find the flesh at fault, blaming the victim
> Of our impatient grab at what is ours,
> Godhead in flesh: and when he came, we sticked him:
> Even after his triumph, our heart cowers.
>
> Will nothing teach us we are freed from sin?
> Still under shame, we think we have to win.

But we must make an observation here. It is quite unhistorical simply to blame the Christian tradition, for the latter merely reflects an erotic incoherence deeply embedded in the culture. Indeed the charge against the Christian tradition here is of its failure to do much more than reflect this incoherence, indeed its tendency to capitalize on it, to say, You are right to be confused, repressive, fearful. The situation is further confused today, in a culture that appears to be anything but confused, repressive, and fearful, but is none the less so. The church's attitude to sexuality mirrors the fear and, above all, the hopelessness, in the culture. We must not mistake the mirror for a beacon. The beacon is Jesus on his cross made revelatory and gracious in Resurrection. The church needs to model her thinking about sexuality on this "dangerous memory" and not on our unconscious negative beliefs about life.

There is a very long history behind this basing of Christian moral doctrine on the bias of the culture. In the fourth century, when Christianity found itself the religion of the empire, it was necessary to elaborate a systematic ethic, and the one at hand was Stoicism. This regarded pleasure as not lawful in itself, only when had in the pursuit of a worthy end. The end, in the case of sexual pleasure, was procreation. Thus—and this is the point—sexual enjoyment did not have its own value, only the permission it got from the real value, procreation. And thus, when sexual moral problems presented themselves, the mutual enjoyment of husband and wife was not among the values that had to be respected and made space for. This lacuna became dramatically evident when, at Vatican II, questions were addressed to the traditional ban on contraception. As we know, the rest is history, and with *Humanae Vitae* the traditional ban was upheld.

Now what the copious discussion that preceded and, even more, followed *Humanae Vitae* brought to light was the intellectual and spiritual poverty of the Catholic tradition on sexuality. A morality evolved by celibates, it showed the fact in failing to see the joy of sex as a crucial factor. So our doctrine on sexuality, at last revealing the bankruptcy of a doctrine based not on Jesus the liberator of desire but on a very narrow human philosophy, is crying out for its true basis, the mystery of Christ crucified and risen.

The present pope is the first pope to attempt this. A few years ago, he devoted his weekly audiences for a whole year to building up a theory of sexuality on the first three chapters of Genesis, read with the eyes of a philosopher and man of profound faith. These talks were edited, paraphrased, and usefully commented upon by Mary Durkin, in a book entitled *Feast of Love: Pope John Paul II on Human Intimacy* (Loyola University Press, 1986).

The fundamental idea behind these talks is that the first three chapters of Genesis, heard with faith, offer a perspective on sexuality that is far wider and deeper than that to which we are accustomed. Further, there is a theological reason why we are accustomed to the narrower view with all the conflicts and contradictions it engenders: the Fall.

What the Fall means, according to Pope John Paul, is that we are very poorly in touch with our sexuality as it truly is, as it images the creating Godhead. To get a glimpse of this true perspective, we have to consider what the story is telling us, first about the deep existential solitude of the human being, which calls us into "partnership with the Absolute," and which reveals the partnership of man and woman as a sharing in this aloneness and partnership with God. Adam's ecstatic cry on seeing the woman—"Behold, bone of my bone, flesh of my flesh!"—is a prelude to the Song of Songs. Of this sublime condition, of intimacy in God, sexual union is the expression. This is the reinstatement of sexual union in its full context, the mystery of our transcendence-oriented and Christ-illuminated humanity. The connecting of Adam's cry "Bone of my bone, flesh of my flesh!" with the lyrics of the Song of Songs is a beautiful poet's touch. We are certainly in a world different from the standard papal pronouncement on sex.

Now the pope stresses with what great difficulty this full meaning of sexuality is realized in our present, fallen condition. And this raises a question: How do we know when we *are* realizing this intimacy with God? In other words, what *is* this full sexual experience? Is there anything in *sex as we know it,* "fallen" though it is, that evidences the beauty of sexual union as a covenantal expression? Or is there only *the idea* of a divinely shaped union, *of* which our sexual experience is the always deficient expression?

I keep getting the feeling, reading these profound reflections, that their author does not believe that there *is* any clue to the sublime reality in sexual experience itself. In reflection on one's body in its maleness or femaleness, its essential incompleteness, yes; in the mysteriousness of the union of two in one flesh, yes. But in *sex,* as we enjoy and suffer it? Somehow, no. That never comes through. This is a phenomenology of sexuality, descriptive of its intentionality. But we are light years away from the world of D. H. Lawrence. I mean that there is no feeling for the area of experience for which Lawrence has found such memorable words. Of course I don't want the pope to write like Lawrence! It's just that when I think of Lawrence, and then read this text, I get the feeling that, though phenomenological and existential, it really is not talking about what Lawrence is talking about at all.

Wondering why this was so, and seeking clues in this dense text, I came upon something that I believe may be the clue. It occurs, not surprisingly, where the moment of the Fall is being explored. John Paul's interpretation of this moment is as follows. The result of disobedience to God is that the harmony, in the human being, between the "higher" and the "lower" nature is lost. It is in the treatment of this lost harmony that I find the clue I have been seeking.

A loss of harmony may—and must, if we are to avoid a fatal distortion—be considered both as a failure of the "lower" to obey the "higher" *and* as a failure of the "higher" to befriend the "lower." But it is only the failure of the "lower" to obey that is considered. For what happens in the pope's account is that they eat the fruit, that is, disobey God, and as a result experience the lustful rebellion of their lower nature, *as a result of which experience* they are filled with shame and cover their sexual organs.

The Genesis story, on the other hand, features the corresponding failure of the "higher" to befriend the "lower." In fact, it makes this failure the key to the whole thing: they eat the fruit, and "immediately their eyes were opened, and they saw that they were naked." Ironically, the would-be god whom the serpent has duped finds the evidences of his/her own animality embarrassing. The thematic connection between shame and the act of disobedience is made no less than three times in the narrative. Before the event, it is said that "they were naked together, and knew no shame." In the event itself, their eyes are opened to their nakedness. And later, in the evening, God says, "Who told you you were naked?" This hubris-inspired embarrassment at being sexual is the experience of the fallen condition. Certainly the "lower nature," thus outlawed, gets its own back by behaving like the outlaw it now is—and this is lust. In other words, it is shame that sets the stage for lust. In the pope's account, it is the other way round: lust generates shame. He insists that "man is ashamed of his body because of lust."

This idea has serious consequences. Shame emerges as an appropriate reaction to the disorder of lust, whereas in the biblical account shame is how sexuality looks to the human pretending to be God; it is the looking down on sexuality that is the immediate effect of claiming divinity as one's own. What disappears from the account of original sin when we follow the pope's order of "shame because of lust" is the notion of sin *consisting in contempt for the flesh*. What is lost to view is that a failure to honor sexual union as an experience is the hubris of original sin. Much of traditional Catholic thinking on sexuality falls into this trap. The "sex, ugh!" of the fallen Adam becomes the "sex, ugh!" of the church. This is that reflecting by the church of the culture's attitude to sex, of which I was speaking just now.

The notion of shame is very tricky. There are the things one ought to be ashamed of, such as cowardice, treachery, lust. And there are the things being ashamed of which indicates a disorder, such as poverty, a humble family background, sexuality. The shame in the Genesis story is clearly and emphatically of the latter sort, and it says so three times. It is precisely the story of how shame comes to be where it should not be. To hear it as talking about a situation where shame *should* be—that is, a lustful situation—is to exclude from consideration just what the story is so forcefully presenting: the inappropriateness, in the divine perspective, of shame to sexuality. What we see of sex, in the story of the Fall as presented by Pope John Paul, is sex as shameful, but not the way the story intends, but rather the way he intends, that is, as shameful because of lust. "Man is ashamed of his body because of lust" is repeated twice in the text. But what the story is saying is that man is ashamed of his body because *it* remains faithful to God in being what it is while man tries to be God. To confuse this latter shame with the shame we appropriately feel over lust, to confuse inappropriate shame with appropriate shame, is ruinous, and grounds the negative view of sexuality out of which the Christian tradition is at last trying to grow.

These profound meditations are seeking in the Genesis account a deeper and truer perspective on sex. Yet at the crucial point where the Fall is dramatized as involving a subtle disesteem of our sexual experience, the implication is missed. What the biblical text can say to us here is not "Sexual experience is not what God meant it to be" but something more like "Beware of downgrading sex in your quest for God. Beware of Neoplatonism. It is not quite Christian."

One of the most significant moments at Vatican II was when the imperative of attention to people's sexual experience as an indispensable unitive value in the human community was thrust upon the representatives of a two-thousand-year-old celibate tradition—when, in other words, the above implication of the story of the Fall became operative in the council's collective mind. The context was the debate on birth control. Could the value enshrined in sexual union be made subservient to a very rigid and long-unquestioned understanding of natural law? Patriarch Maximos, an octogenarian, suggested that church authority suffered from a "bachelor psychosis." Cardinal Suenens warned the fathers that we might, if we persisted in the traditional attitude to contraception, have another Galileo case on our hands, which might be one too many. And Charles Davis, a *peritus* at the council, told the press that evening, "Today, my role as a theologian changed."

The plunge was not taken. The birth control question was taken out of the council's hands and given to a papal commission, whose virtually unanimous vote for change was ignored. Not one of the small minority against change upheld the traditional doctrine. Their only argument was, "If we change, no one will ever believe in the authority of the church again," a prophecy ironically fulfilled by what has followed the decision *not* to change. It has been demonstrated sociologically that a far greater exodus of people from the American church can be traced to the encyclical *Humanae Vitae* than to any other of the many possible factors of our changing time.

In sum, the reason the pope's biblical mirror to sexuality does not show sexual experience as we know it, fallen though we are, as valid and revelatory of God, is that where the biblical text shows our fallenness to consist precisely in the downgrading of sexuality, with which we are only too familiar, the pope does not follow the text. On the contrary, by inverting the text's order of shame and lust, he gets *from* the text a downgrading of sexual experience. He sees the downgrading of sexual experience as *justified* by the fact of the Fall, whereas this downgrading *is* the Fall in its immediate effect. In short, he reads the text as justifying the attitude which the text is telling us we must deplore.

This is really the crux of the matter. The split between the lower and the higher nature happens in losing touch with the mystery I am in. That is to say, it is an *attitudinal* split. It is what the world gets to feel like when I am no longer in the mystery. The story captures this "consequential attitude" beautifully: "and immediately their eyes were opened." This means that "what the world looks like"—sexuality alienated and untrustworthy, for instance—is an illusion consequent upon the deepest alienation. It is not a new normative state of affairs. Original sin is not a regime. It is not a new quasi nature superimposed on the original. It is something we have to *allow for,* and massively, in our assessment of social and political situations—indeed it can turn politics into something like a dramatized lie, as in current electioneering—but it is not something to be *consulted.* To treat it as a regime is to succumb to it.

The Council of Trent fought to maintain the goodness of nature despite the Fall, against the tragic Christianity of the reformers. It is perhaps the acid test of

Catholicity, closely allied with the dearly held con-
sonance of faith with reason. But it needs to be recovered today in the context of a much more subjective
understanding of the human condition. Any notion of
original sin suggesting that it is a new norm resists this
necessary advance into ever-living and unchanging
truth.

I am not saying we can undo the Fall. I am saying that
we have to learn from it, and that we do not learn from
it by promoting the very attitude of shame at sex that
results from the Fall. A correct reading of the text will
demote, not promote, this attitude. Of course sexual
shame is part and parcel of our condition. But a theology that fails to see farther than this is not faithful to
"the oracles of God."

And I am not saying that any casual sexual experience
is revelatory of God. I am saying that where sexual
experience *is* so revelatory, it is so in the delightful way it
happens, and not in the deep speculations of philosophy. This is the crux, of course. Whenever the Vatican
talks of sex, it never seems to have in mind what people
experience as sex, what they experience sex as. The gulf
is always there. It was very nearly bridged at that historic
moment during Vatican II, to which I have referred.

It is perhaps because this interpretation of Genesis
reinstates, reestablishes, this gulf between the sexual
reality and sexual theologizing, that the present pope
has felt able to reverse the trend that followed *Humanae
Vitae,* namely, the benign attitude of some national hierarchies to contraception, which has been authority's way
of admitting, at last, the laity's experience as crucial in
this whole affair. The sharp difference between the tone
of Pius XI's *Casti Connubii* (1930) and that of the national
hierarchies following the birth-control encyclical has not
been sufficiently marked—least of all by the hierarchies

themselves! It must be recalled, now that the supreme
authority seems to be recovering the confidence of *Casti
Connubii.* To anyone who is wondering how this can be
happening, I would commend a close study of this profound text.

Nevertheless, with this text of a reigning pope, an
important step is taken toward the recognition of sexual
desire as an ethical value. And amidst all the press
hoopla let loose by his statement that husbands should
not lust after their wives, no one noticed that, for the
first time in church history surely, a reigning pontiff was
admitting that rape could happen in marriage. But the
step was not completed, and the effect of this, curiously,
is to reinforce the position before the step was taken. In
the larger context of a millennial position based on
Stoicism, the step was a momentous one, and this may
account for the retreat. Feeling the heat of the fire, the
hand is sharply withdrawn.

So the step has still to be taken. Only when it is, only
when sexual desire is understood, by that massively
powerful force Catholic tradition, in the light of Christianity's and humanity's central mystery, will the church
be empowered to critique the appalling sexual derailment of our time. And the role of the Petrine office,
which is to bring together the huge creative forces in
Christianity, needs to be exercized here. It may turn out
that one advantage of modern secularism, a good blown
by this otherwise ill wind, is to render no longer attrac-
tive the pursuit of ecclesiastical power, which is the main
obstacle to the emergence of the massive spiritual power
of the church centered in Rome, the only worldwide
and world-old institution that is committed to changing
the world.

Once the step is taken, discrimination occurs. Sexual
desire is no longer seen in a primitive and undifferenti-

ated way as a powerful force that has to be curbed, but as a value that needs to be fostered. For desire as personal and person-oriented is not something automatic. On the contrary, it requires patient labor involving the deep differences between man and woman. "The difference between [me and my husband]," said a woman to psychologist Lillian Rubin, "is that for me foreplay begins at breakfast." The axiom explored earlier in this book, that real desire desires its own increase and is spiritual ("pneumatic") and not easily discovered in oneself, applies above all to sexuality. The most dramatic, indeed comic, instance of cross-purposes between the Vatican and the married, is that the Vatican sees the problem as one of curbing desire, whereas the married know that the problem is to keep desire going, which means to keep it growing, which means deepening. As Andrew Greeley puts it, the Vatican warns against "unbridled passion." When will they realize that the problem with most marriages is bridled passion? We all desire to be desired by one we desire, but the fulfillment of this longing involves much dying to ego. It is nothing less than the transition from the way ego wants to be desired—the ego still pursuing its childhood agenda—to the realization of my desirableness as a person, as a creature, as a body, as a disclosure of God. It means coming to that desire which flows out of the fullness of my being in the mystery that grounds all that is.

Finally, a word about St. Augustine. It is customary to lay the blame for much of the church's negative view of sexuality on St. Augustine. We all know Rosemary Reuther's protest to the effect that fifteen centuries dominated by the problem of Augustine's penis is enough. Actually, the way Augustine relates lust to original sin looks very like the notion I am using in critiquing Pope John Paul's notion of lust, for he sees sexual lust as a *subset* of the much more fundamental *libido dominandi* ("the impulse to dominate"). In other words, it derives from that trying to be God that is the essence of the Fall. And there is not all that difference between contempt for sexuality and the use of sexuality to further one's ego-project. Lust, then, is not sexual passion out of the control of the will, but sexual passion acting as a cover-story for the will to be God.

This is well illustrated in Iris Murdoch's recent novel *The Good Apprentice*. Harry Cuno has an affair going with Midge, the wife of Tom McCaskerville. The affair has lasted two years, and Harry is bringing enormous pressure on Midge to tell Tom, get a divorce, and start a "real" marriage with him. After Murdoch, in her inimitable way, has had events shake up the human kaleidescope, the pieces settle with Midge deciding that she really does love Tom and their twelve-year-old Meredith, and she tells Harry. The latter responds with a series of letters in which the rhetoric of passion excels itself. He writes, "I cannot and will not accept what you say. Please be clear about this. I will not accept it and you do not mean it. This is, how strange, my first love letter to you," and much more in this vein. Finally Midge replies with a single line, "No. I am sorry. No." And then Harry realizes, quite simply, that he has lost. And then comes the vague thought that there will be others. The hounds of passion have been called off by the ego, which thus reveals that it has been calling the shots all along. His love turns out to have been an extremely sophisticated form of lust.

So I'm inclined to say, "Hands off Augustine!" (In general, we've got to get beyond this trendy theology, Elaine Pagels and all that.) He tasted God, and while this did not result, as with Rabbi Akiba, in his getting sex straight, it did teach him that getting sex wrong came from trying to *be* God; that lust means not getting sex straight, and does not just mean letting sex rip. He cannot be invoked as the perpetrator of the great anomaly, of a desire that joins man to woman and creates the human future, yet of whose *intrinsic* holiness no account is given, whose need to be joined with deep life-commitment is insisted upon while the relational nature of this desire which *leads* it to seek commitment is not clarified; the anomaly, in short, of a lyric about which the only language we have is the language of control, of a hedonistic God proclaimed by a forbidding church.

The task before us is not to subject sexual passion to the will, but to restore it to desire, whose origin and end is God, whose liberation is of God's grace made manifest in the life, teaching, crucifixion, and Resurrection of Jesus Christ.

> The wonder of arousal
> Has never ceased to be
> A source of speculation
> Whose place is he and she.
>
> Long before man or woman
> Were lettered, self-aware,
> Passion arose between them
> Of quality so rare:
>
> Alone among the passions
> This one was ecstasy:
> Alone it made two persons
> Dream of eternity.
>
> These two characteristics,
> Pleasure and permanence,
> Stood out, and holy mystics
> Joined them without offense.
>
> Most have preferred to keep them
> In line as best they could,
> Which wasn't very well—still
> We must try to be good.

> The Church that pushed our thinking
> In other regions far,
> In this one was most timid,
> Her preference to bar.
>
> Why ecstasy seeks bonding
> She did not ask, invoked
> Rather her power God-given
> To keep the couple yoked.
>
> The anomaly stays with us,
> Stays our becoming whole:
> A high, God-given lyric
> Whose language is control.
>
> Unplumbed is the resentment
> Of those who know the joy
> And hear the Church propounding
> As though it were a toy.

But the discovery of sexuality in the light of desire seeking liberation in Christ is part of a wider strategy of recovery and discovery. In the next chapter, we shall ask the more far-reaching questions, How may we liberate the mind from the traps in which our senescent Western culture is caught? What are the traps? How did we get into them? How do we get out of them?

11

Liberating the Modern Mind

There is an account of the human significance of science
that is very common among religious believers, and
often remains implicit. It goes like this. Science is essentially the attempt to dominate the world we live in. It
assumes a Godlike stance in relation to the world. In so
doing, it reduces the world from a circumambient mystery, which it is, to a vast system of dead matter in
motion, the Newtonian universe so detested by Blake
and dubbed by him the Land of Ulro. Religious recovery, runs this account, is the recovery of the myths
whereby we lived before the age of science. (The re-
markable popularity of Joseph Campbell's television series is evidence of this attitude.)

This account, I believe, is built on a mistaken notion
of the human significance of science. Underlying the
scientific revolution represented by Galileo and Coper-
nicus and many others, there is a change in our attitude
to the world. It consists in the realization that everything
in the world is intelligible. Aquinas believed as much,
but he could not know the *taste* of what he believed, in
terms of tangible things obeying elegant mathematical
laws, the taste that intoxicated the pioneers of the new
age. For the first time, it felt for real that everything in
the universe, be it ever so odd and challenging, is open

to the lucky insight, the derived hypothesis, and the verifiable proposition.

Now how do we *know* that everything that is or could be is intelligible? You might say that we know this as a daring *why not?* inspired by some successful foray into a hitherto unexplored realm. One can imagine Newton saying, "Dammit, the whole thing must be like this, like gravity was before I discovered it." But this hunch is only the first stirring of a new certainty that is in the very nature of mind. The mind is awakening to itself. Everything is dependent on God; everything is intelligible to mind. A vital rhyme is felt between these two statements. For Eckhart, mind can see the world as God sees it.

The discovery was not new. Aquinas knew it when he said that the "light of agent intellect," that in us which can make everything understood, is a participation in the divine light. What was dramatically new was the *realization* of this Godlike stance of mind in relation to the whole universe. So intense in fact was the drama of it, that it distracted attention from the new light within, which was its source.

And it is ever thus. Few people ever stop to ask the generic wonder questions: How come there is anything at all? Why am I me? How come we know anything at all? At crucial moments in human development, the asking, in the new context, of the wonder questions makes the difference between advance and derailment. In the moment we are considering, the question was, Who are we, that we know the whole world is intelligible? It indicates a disturbingly new intimacy to the drama of finite and infinite, the discovery of the self as the stage on which this drama is set.

Let us recall a saying of Einstein, "The most incomprehensible thing about the universe is that it is comprehensible." If that statement leaps out at you, you know exactly what I am talking about. It is one of those brilliant observations that make perfect sense on Mondays and Thursdays, and go dead on other days. What he finds overwhelming—"incomprehensible"—is not the universe in all its vastness, but the unaccountable and undeniable certainty that the whole thing can make sense. What he finds awesome is the divine light that is being experienced in the mind when a new degree of maturity has banished the gods whose caprices used to account for what happened, and stepped into a totally comprehensible universe. He is registering, in a brilliantly paradoxical way, the new step I have referred to, whereby the subordination of everything to God the Unknown is reflected in the openness of everything to the inquiring mind. In Einstein's observation, we feel the scientific revolution on the pulse of the mind where it has the character of a theophany.

It should now appear what a disastrous mistake it is to define modern science as the attempt to play God, when its governing insight is a new experience of the light of God; to *deplore* the Godlike stance of science that is in fact a new realization of the Godlike nature of the human being. With the scientific revolution, the Judeo-Christian insight into the human being as in the image of God achieves a new and brilliant verification, so that Herbert Butterfield could say that it is the greatest thing that has happened since the coming of Christianity.

The tragedy has been that this crucial insight that underlies the scientific revolution has not been attended to. Thus an amazing opportunity to grow up in God, to know God as the mind's light, has been missed. And of course, once you concentrate on the achievements of science at the expense of the insight, then you do fall into hubris. To fail to see hubris as the distortion of science, and to make of it the essence of science, is an example of "playing the tune badly, and concluding thence that it's a bad tune."

And the main casualty is our way of thinking about God. Denied its new and spacious habitat in the growing mind as it comes into a new relationship with the cosmos, it is exiled into a pietism that underlies the sterile conflict between science and religion, and, at the limit, a know-nothing fascistic fundamentalism.

A very important recent book shows in great historical detail how the Christian apologists and theologians contributed to this major oversight. In *At the Origins of Modern Atheism,* Michael Buckley, S.J., shows how Christian thinkers were so impressed with the newly structured universe that they thought of God as the architect of this great scheme. They forgot God as known in the Christian tradition of prayer, community, and sacrament, and came to mean by "God" the Great Mathematician. They invested everything in the "argument from design," which has always been a poor relation in the Christian apologetic—St. Thomas does not use it at all. When, a few generations later, scientific thinkers came to see that there was no need for this Great Mathematician, the Christian apologists found themselves with nowhere to stand. The result is that atheism and academic respectability are synonymous, and the occasional believer on a philosophical faculty comes to feel like a devotee of the horoscope.

I have a question for Fr. Buckley, however. What were these new scientific Christian apologists turning their backs on in their excited pursuit of a new apologetic? He would say, "on the whole broad and deep traditional sense of God in church and sacrament," and this is surely true. But weren't they also failing to see—and is this not the point?—the new theological implication *in the scientific movement itself,* namely the self-discovery of mind as revelatory of God in its newfound certainty of being able to come to understand everything in the universe, the genial insight of Einstein in that great saying? The scientific revolution was not merely a challenge not to forget the mystical in tradition. It was an invitation to a further appropriation of the mystical. The scientific banishing of the gods was—although this was not realized—a deepening of the Judeo-Christian insight into the one God, whose image is not the sacred grove but the human being from whose mind nothing in the cosmos is withheld.

Now it is only when, harkening to what Einstein is saying, we are dumbfounded by our position as the mind of the universe, that the beyond that we call God gets its real meaning. The beyond is within. It is no longer beyond what is out there, behind the ingenuity of birds and reptiles. It is *really* beyond, reached for by the self-questioning of this world-knowing being. Beyond is beyond me.

And what is beyond me? Nothing finite, nothing that could be defined, in short, nothing at all. For as far back as Aristotle, we knew the mind as "able to make and become all things." Beyond me, then, is only the infinite—provided the "me" we are talking about is the self awakened to its power to understand all, the self that underwent this awakening with new vividness when modern science was born. Beyond one to whom everything is intelligible, there is only the infinite. Before we know ourselves, in our Godlike stance toward everything, *beyond* means *behind* what we *don't* understand—hence the argument from design, called by Richard Dawkins the argument from personal incomprehension. In his brilliant book *The Blind Watchmaker,* Dawkins counts fifty instances where Hugh Montefiore says, "Further, one does not see how," etc. With our coming into our center whence all may be understood, we know the real beyond that is infinite. Lonergan makes this point superbly when he says, "God is not the explanation of anything: God is the explanation of explanation."

Now once we have sensed in this way the real meaning of *beyond*, we understand the meaning of desire. For desire *is* a going beyond what is, to what could be. And we have already considered that, at the crucial moments of desire's going beyond what is, the ego has to undergo death to accommodate this new reach of desire. The meaning of this trajectory of reaching beyond, from its infant beginnings to its consummation, is known when we know ourselves, our spiritual unboundedness, as having the beyond that is infinity itself.

There is an intriguing parallel between the early scientific revolution, with its attendant oversight, and the revolution initiated by Freud, which also is accompanied by an oversight. Freud recovered for a thoroughly rationalistic generation the reality of myth as expressive of a perennial human dynamic. He found inexorably working itself out in the lives of his civilized patients the ancient myth of Oedipus. And Jung vastly expanded the mythic world that shows itself to our dreams. But the unavowed inspiration of this revolution is an understanding of myth that is quite new, namely, as a function of self-realization. A new subject is implied, for whom the world of myth no longer expresses a dark law by which our lives are bound, but is a challenge to become ourselves. Thus both the revolution in cosmology and the revolution in psychology have a hidden, unacknowledged nerve: a new coming-to-itself of the human being. And in both cases, the human comes to him- or herself *as* somehow *above* the world of nature and the world of psyche, to both of which a less self-aware humanity felt itself to be subject. And in both cases what is implied is a dramatically new opening up of the beyond. If I am beyond this world, what is beyond me?

So what is needed for our healing is the reclaiming of that new sense of self opened beyond itself that is the unacknowledged source of our two major revolutions, cosmological and psychological. What I started this chapter by critiquing would be, by contrast, a retreat from the cosmological revolution misunderstood into the psychic world also misunderstood.

What all this means is that we can have an experiential knowledge of our orientation toward the infinite. We have this when the *intellectual* component of our all-reaching, learned in the cosmological revolution, is enfleshed in the *existential* component, learned in the psychological revolution. And then we get a sense of the central thrust of desire which is *at once* the desire to know and the desire to be in love. It is not surprising, then, that the Holy Spirit, the instigator and consummation of desire, should be associated indifferently with love and wisdom. The Holy Spirit is, as I have already suggested, the healing of that dichotomy between knowing and loving of which our world is dying. We can have some antecedent understanding of that healing in the full elucidation of desire.

Thus the two primary needs of our time are the recovery of mythic awareness (the psychological revolution releasing its real meaning) and the recovery of the power to transcend myth (the cosmological revolution releasing its real meaning). The compassing of this double end is not easy, since those who are most helpful with the mythic dimension—the Jungs, the Joseph Campbells, the Robert Blys—tend to be woolly on transcendence. And conversely, it is difficult to get the intellectually converted to attend to their dreams.

But the two *want* to come together. The human eros seeks meaning in the whole world of our archetypes, and stretches beyond that world into incomprehensible mystery via the discovered incompetence of reason in that domain. It is all one eros, as there is one Holy Spirit that transforms it. In a final chapter, I shall look at some exciting signs in post-Freudian psychology of the discovery of desire as one in its emotional and its intellectual thrust.

12

A Paradigm Shift in Contemporary Psychology

The history of psychoanalysis since Freud is instructive, for it shows a growing dissatisfaction with the fundamental assumption of modernity, that the person is to be regarded as a monad—analogously, an organism—whose dysfunctioning it is the task of therapy to remedy. The discovery that babies wilt and die for lack of relatedness—that even in our earliest beginnings we do not live by bread alone—led to the development of object-relations theory. The coming and thriving of family therapy pointed in the same direction, of the person as a relatedness. Most important has been D. W. Winnicott's concept of the transitional object. The teddybear, and certain cherished rituals, are reminders, tokens, of life in the womb. These tokens, fondled out in the cold world, carry forward into that world the warmth of our earlier enclosure.

It is when we ask precisely what function the transitional object is performing, that a new development suggests itself. I am indebted for the following crucial insight to a recent lecture by John McDargh.

It has been assumed that what the infant, and later the grown person, is fundamentally about is *surviving* intact. How can I, this lonely individual who looks back to a preconscious envelopment in the comfort of the womb, survive in this harsh world? But suddenly it occurs to me that this is looking at the thing inside out. The huge overall scientist bias has got us thinking of man the lonely explorer, dealing with a strange world out there, and this image has inserted itself into the way we envisage the infant dealing with the world. He "negotiates" the new situation like an astronaut faced with an unexpected challenge ("Houston, we have a problem, it's horribly lonely out here!"). But does not everything suggest that it's exactly the other way around, that the infant is *being drawn* into even fuller life in the world? Far from an essentially lonely being trying to find its way in alien territory, the infant becomes a total relatedness wanting to enter into and consciously enjoy more and more of these implicit relationships. The desire that impels him is not, in the last analysis, the need to be comfortable, to be stable, to survive, but rather the desire to be knowingly in this infinitely exciting world that reveals itself more and more with each passing day and that, as soon as language begins to be acquired, provokes an infinity of questions, themselves the carriers of desire. And it is noted that, even in its earliest weeks, a baby will interrupt feeding to explore a new development in the world of brightly colored things.

A new paradigm is emerging, under the growing pressure of observations that fit less and less easily into the old one. I am not a monad, seeking to keep comfortable and to survive. I am a relatedness all around, seeking to actualize more and more this relatedness. It is this need to connect more and more, to go out more and more, that is painfully frustrated in an oppressed childhood, not just the need to feel comfortable. Unrequited love is a very early and fateful experience, that I have already connected with shame.

It is this effort of my relatedness to become actual, and not the attempt to be comfortable, that gives to desire its fundamental nature. Reality draws me into itself. It does not stand over against me, opposing its harsh "reality principle" to my secret "pleasure principle." My pleasure principle is an infinite curiosity responding to the allure of the real.

Now to say that desire is for my relatedness to the world to become actual is to say something new about desire and to say something new about knowing. It is to connect desire with coming-to-know, and it is to connect knowing with desire. And it was in the context of this radical revision of Freud that I suddenly saw in a new way the importance of the work of Bernard Lonergan. The one thing that everyone who reads or hears about Lonergan comes away with—the first thing that attracted me to him forty years ago—is that "knowing is not taking a look." What I just came to see is that Lonergan's overhaul of cognitional process is not just a philosophical affair. It strikes at the roots of all our cultural assumptions. The modern mind is shaped by the assumption that we are *confronted* by the real—the astronaut confronted by the strange things out there—and that knowing consists in taking in this alien baggage. Reviving an understanding as old as philosophy, Lonergan says that initially we are *one* with the real, and that knowing is a coming to differentiate within that oneness, and, most importantly, that the process of knowing is started by becoming interested in images that are born out of our oneness with the world—remember the tiny baby interrupting feeding to consider the colored things. And images are the crystallizing of desires, as all dream therapy recognizes. What Lonergan is awakening us to is, that the opposition we take for granted between desiring and knowing, between dream and reality, between the desirable and the actual, between pleasure principle and reality principle, is false.

With this, a flood of dammed-up energy is released. The deep split in our culture between head and heart begins to mend. Knowing is different—it is desire coming to fulfillment. Desire is different—it stretches out to know. We hardly know ourselves as these two mutually estranged parts of our mind embrace. And we hardly know where to begin the total reconstitution of our world that this embrace entails. But we begin to understand why Scripture sees the Holy Spirit as "dilating the heart"—in love? in wisdom? What is the difference? We understand why the Pharisaic sin to which the Gospel is primary opposed is the sin of not seeing. We begin to see why the main tradition sees the beatific *vision* as our goal. The theological school that contradicts this, saying that love was the goal, was already making the split between knowing and loving that has proved so ruinous. The fourteenth century saw the collapse of the medieval synthesis, so that there was no longer a healthy mind ready to digest the prodigious discoveries that were just around the corner.

And we can attach new meaning to Paul's description of our end as "knowing as I am known." I am a total relatedness waiting and wanting to be realized. We might explain this condition of being a total relatedness as a condition of being totally known. For it implies a total intelligibility in me that is in an infinite mind but hardly at all in me. I am totally connected up without my appreciating all this connectedness. What then will be the actualization of this total relatedness, the entry into who I am? It will be coming "to know as I am known." But we have seen that *desire* is for the actualizing of our relatedness. It is desire that draws us into who we really are. Therefore desire is wanting to known as I am known. I desire to be knowingly in the total relatedness of which I am constituted. The following two sonnets attempt to express, respectively, Lonergan's great insight in its full emotional context, and the fuller notion of desire with which this chapter is concerned.

> Knowing is looking, is what most philosophers
> Assume. Reality is there. We bump it.
> And what is there, intractable, deters
> Our flights of fancy: we just have to lump it.
>
> And so the world of dreams and that of fact
> Stand in stark opposition: our desires
> Encounter the real world, against them stacked.
> Pleasure before reality retires.
>
> Yet knowing is not looking, but desire
> At one with world, conceiving images
> For insight; then reflection and the spir-
> al sweep of knowing puts the mind at ease.
>
> If knowing is desire rising to light,
> Dreams and reality don't have to fight.

This one I call "De Sideribus" ("Out of the Stars") because this is probably the etymology of *desiderium*:

> Desire to know even as I am known:
> That *is* desire, creation coming conscious,
> Amoeba growing out to all, its own,
> The maggot Israel illustrious.
>
> The infant interrupts the flow of warm
> Milk to observe a change in the world scene:
> Eyes opening, lips parted to the charm,
> Islands of ecstasy where we have been.

Desire is to relax into what is,
The unknown knowing one, the dance in three,
Heart of the universe an open kiss
Opens our private worlds so we are we.

Desire indeed is the desire to know,
For we are known, and into this we grow.